The Promise

PAT NICHOLS

The Promise by Pat Nichols
Published by Armchair Press
ISBN:979-8-9912411-2-0
Copyright © 2025 by Pat Nichols
Cover Design by Elaina Lee
Edited by Sherri Stewart

Available in print from your local bookstore or online.
For more information on this book or the author visit:
https://patnicholsauthor.blog
Printed in the United States of America
The Promise is a work of fiction. Names, characters, and incidents are all products of the author's imagination or are used for fictional purposes. Any mentioned brand names, places, and trademarks remain the property of their respective owners, bear no association with the author or publisher, and are used for fictional purposes only.
Library of Congress Cataloging-in Publication Data
Nichols, Pat.
The Promise / Pat Nichols

All rights reserved. No portion of this book may be reproduced in any form, stored in a retrieval system, or transmitted in any form by any means—electronic, photocopy, recording, or otherwise—without written permission from the publisher or author, except as permitted by U.S. copyright law.

Books by
Pat Nichols

Women's Fiction

Blue Ridge Series

Blizzard at Blue Ridge Inn
The Inheritance
The Wedding
Christmas at Hilltop Inn
The Promise
Summer of Second Chances
More titles in 2025

Willow Falls Series

The Secret of Willow Inn
Trouble in Willow Falls
Starstruck in Willow Falls
Bridges, Books, and Bones

Butler Family LegacySeries

Big Secrets, Little Lies
Truth and Forgiveness
New Beginnings

Dedicated to beta readers, Pat Davis and Bev Feldkamp who have traveled with me on my author journey from the beginning.

Chapter 1

Wendy stashed the two empty suitcases in the closet and closed the door then stepped onto the top-floor balcony. Rain pummeled the multi-faceted glass roof covering the lush atrium, but failed to dampen her spirits as she peered down at the green oasis stretching below Nashville's Gaylord Opryland. Such a welcome sight in the dead of winter. "Our first vacation as a family."

Chris held their eight-month-old son in his arms. "The first of many."

Wendy fingered her Christmas gift from Chris, a ring featuring a pale blue stone partially encircled with a curved row of leaf-shaped diamonds. "The only other balcony you and I stood on overlooked the Atlantic Ocean."

"Where I asked you to marry me and make me the happiest man alive." A smile lit Chris's face. "One day when our children are old enough to appreciate the experience, we'll visit countries on the other side of the Atlantic."

Resisting the urge to run her fingers through Chris's thick brown hair, she stuffed her hands in her pockets. "Is this your way of telling me you're eager to give our little guy a baby brother or sister?"

"One reason Allison and I are close is because we're only two years apart." Chris's eyes met Wendy's. "We'll work on expanding our family when the time is right for you."

"Hmm." A delicious tingling sensation surged through Wendy's limbs. "If we conceive this weekend, do you suppose our baby will end up a Georgia or a Tennessee football fan?"

He winked. "Definitely Georgia."

A bird flew past their balcony then perched on a branch. Wendy's focus drifted down from the tree to a man holding a young child's hand as they strolled along the winding path. How would her father have responded if he had discovered he'd fathered a child twenty-three years before she and Chris showed up at his house? "Do you suppose Douglas Hewitt has given me even a fleeting thought since our trip to Hilton Head?"

"Well—"

"You don't need to respond, darling."

"A hypothetical question?"

Wendy nodded. "The truth is the man who drank too much during spring break and had a one-night fling with Cynthia will never be part of my family or my life." Wendy plucked her pinging phone off the glass table. "Speaking of family. Kayla's waiting for me in the lobby."

"An hour earlier than we expected her to show up."

"She probably skipped a couple of classes. Which means our make-a-baby party will have to wait for a few more hours."

Chris brushed a lock of blonde hair away from her face. "Definitely a party well worth waiting for."

"Maybe I'll splurge and buy something special to wear." Wendy kissed her son's cheek. "Your daddy will take good care of you while I catch up with your secret cousin." She grabbed her phone then stepped inside.

After pocketing the room key and a credit card, Wendy walked out and turned right. She arrived at the elevator bank, her mind drifting to the only other time she had come to Nashville—the day she showed up uninvited at her mother's house.

An elevator door yawned open. Wendy stepped in, faced the front, and leaned on the back wall. She stared at the numbers above the door as images from that day played in her mind. Cynthia's stunned expression the moment she realized Wendy was the daughter she hadn't seen in eighteen years. Sitting in the Gilmores' formal living room beside Amanda, her business partner who'd come along for moral support. The array of family photos that mocked her from the white baby grand piano. The cold-hearted way her mother rationalized abandoning her five-year-old and never telling her new family that her first-born child existed. Wendy's breath caught when the elevator stopped at lobby level. She stepped out.

Kayla rushed to embrace her. "You picked a cool place for us to meet."

Wendy peered over her half-sister's shoulder. "Are you alone?"

"Uh-huh." Kayla released her. "My friend Harper dropped me off on the way to her part-time job."

Wendy's eyes widened. "Instead of your boyfriend?"

"We broke up. He turned out to be kind of a jerk."

Relieved the older kid was out of the picture, Wendy looped her hand around Kayla's elbow as they headed toward the atrium. "Do you hang out at Opryland a lot?"

"Not really. Last Christmas, Dad brought us here for ICE."

"What's ICE?"

"An indoor winter wonderland—perfect for little kids. Afterwards we ate at Old Hickory Steakhouse."

"Chris and I have dinner reservations at Cascades. I hope you can stay long enough to join us."

"Dad won't be home until way past midnight, and my brother and sister are sleeping over at friends' houses. So I can stay here with you, but you'll need to take me home or call an Uber."

At least her mother wouldn't recognize Chris's car when Wendy dropped her off. "We'll drive you." Wendy released Kayla's elbow. At least her half-sister seemed in a good mood, but then fifteen-year-olds were difficult to read. Should she ask what was going on with their mother's health situation? Maybe she should begin with a safer subject. "How's everything going at school?"

"Okay, I guess." Kayla paused. "Except I'm sort of failing algebra."

So much for a safe topic. "What do you mean by sort of?"

"D minus on my last test. I suppose it doesn't matter all that much, since I'll never need to know how to do equations."

"Do you remember me telling you I had the same opinion until I became Awesam's chief financial officer?"

"Yeah, when you discovered you're a numbers whiz. That doesn't apply to me because I'll never take a job that requires any sort of math." Kayla fell silent for a long moment. "Do you mind if I ask a personal question?"

How personal? Wendy's brow pinched then released. "I'm listening."

"I've been wondering why you call our mother Cynthia. Is it because you hate her for abandoning you?"

A knot gripped Wendy's gut. Hate was such a powerful emotion. She owed her sister the truth. "Although I've forgiven her, Cynthia's rejecting me when I was five and again last year has left deep emotional scars that—even after all these years—are difficult to overcome."

"If she had abandoned me, I don't know if I could've forgiven her." Kayla slowed her pace and moved to the railing. "Mom's thinner than she was a couple of months ago. Some days she doesn't have enough energy to fix dinner."

Not a good sign. Wendy moved beside her half-sister.

"I still don't understand why she and Dad refuse to tell us kids what's wrong with her."

Wendy peered down at the man-made river snaking through the atrium. What did Kayla expect from the woman who kept her oldest daughter's existence a secret? How would Cynthia react if she found out about her relationship with Kayla? Tilting her head up, Wendy scanned the hotel's top floor. Chris sat on their balcony with Ryan on his knee. Had he spotted them?

"Maybe it's time to tell Mom that you and I have a relationship."

Wendy's back stiffened. Conflicting emotions reeled inside. She blew a long stream of air. It couldn't end well especially if Cynthia was sick, but if that's what Kayla wanted, Wendy should at least have the courage to support her. "Do you want me to go with you and tell her tonight?"

Her secret sister shook her head. "Mom's spending tonight and the next three days at her best friend's lake house."

Relief washed over Wendy. "Maybe another time."

Kayla spun away from the railing. "Know what I wanna do now?"

"Check out some shops?"

"How'd you know?"

Wendy linked arms with her sister. "I'm a recovered shopaholic."

Kayla's eyes widened. "Really?"

"Big time."

While making their way toward the shops, Wendy shared stories of the shopping habit she had adopted during the three years she'd lived with Gunter before she discovered they weren't legally married.

Kayla yanked her arm away from Wendy and pointed to the Cowboys and Angels sign. "We have to go in that store."

"Because cowboys are cool?"

"And because Chris calls you 'Angel.' Come on." Kayla raced ahead.

Wendy followed her into the upscale space displaying a wide array of cowboy and cowgirl attire—not her style, but fun. Especially for Nashville.

After browsing through a rack of shirts, Kayla plucked a tan cowgirl hat off a display and fingered the beaded turquoise band. "This one's cool."

"Why don't you go ahead and try it on."

"Okay." Kayla popped the hat on her head and stepped in front of a mirror. "What do you think?"

Wendy nodded. "Definitely you." She donned the same color hat with a different band then stood beside her sister.

"We both make good cowgirls."

"Which is why you and I need matching hats."

"Really?"

"Uh-huh. Besides, I promised Chris I'd buy something fun to wear tonight." Wendy giggled as she imagined wearing nothing other than a cowgirl hat for their private party. "Although I doubt this is what he had in mind."

"At least he'll be surprised."

"For sure." Wendy pulled her credit card from her pocket. After paying for both items, she and Kayla made their way back to the atrium. Following a half-hour stroll amid chats about Nashville's music scene, they settled on a bench at the end of a path. A waterfall spilled over boulders and splashed into the pool below.

Kayla plucked a dead leaf off the bench. "Did you know Mom dreamed of becoming a famous singer?"

"She told me about that the one time I visited her at your house."

"Maybe chasing her dream was the reason she gave you away and married Dad."

Wendy's heart ached as she peered at her sister's downcast eyes. "Childhood dreams give children who grow up in poverty hope for a brighter future."

"Except Mom's not poor anymore." Kayla crushed the leaf then peeled back her fingers and let the pieces flutter to the pavement. "I know she doesn't much like being a mother." Her tone screamed of pain.

Wendy scooted closer to her sister. "Maybe she doesn't know how to show her love."

"A mother can't show love she doesn't feel." Kayla fingered the ruby ring encircled with diamonds on her right hand. "Even though Mom gave me her favorite ring…I feel closer to you than I've ever felt to her."

Wendy swallowed the fist-sized lump forming in her throat. "Because we're sisters."

Kayla focused on her folded hands. "I see how you are with your son. The way you love on Ryan is how mothers are supposed to treat their children. If Mom had paid half as much attention to me—" Tears welled and spilled down Kayla's cheeks.

Wendy slid her arm around her sister's trembling shoulders.

She sniffed. "The only reason my sister and brother exist is because Dad wanted a big family. If he had known about you all those years ago, he wouldn't have let her abandon you." Kayla swiped her fingers across her face. "I'm glad I found the letter Mom secretly wrote to you last year."

"So am I." Wendy's phone pinged a text. "Chris will meet us at the restaurant in ten minutes."

"Perfect timing." Kayla swiped at her cheeks again and popped up. "I'm starving."

Chris met them at the entrance to the outdoor restaurant at the edge of a massive pond. He kissed Wendy's cheek, then placed Ryan in her arms and hugged Kayla. "Cool hats."

"A gift from Wendy. She told me you expected her to buy something fancy to wear tonight."

"Indeed, I did." Chris winked at Wendy.

She could feel her face heat up.

A hostess escorted them to a table overlooking the water. Kayla seemed mesmerized by streams of water shooting between rock islands lush with vegetation and lights submerged in pools. Wendy's eyes met Chris's. "A couple of weeks before Valentine's Day is the perfect time to celebrate the love we all have for each other."

Kayla pulled her phone from her pocket, then posed between Wendy and Chris and snapped a picture. "My secret family."

Chapter 2

Following three days of intense courtroom drama and two hours of tension-laced debate in the jury deliberation room, Erica's head pounded with pain. Tagged as Juror Number Nine among five women and seven men, she had maintained a measure of calm until the defense attorney called his first witness. The woman's response to his second question peeled back protective layers of a memory which had remained buried deep in Erica's subconscious for nearly three decades. The longer the witness talked, the more the forgotten memory spiraled to the surface. If that wasn't enough, why did something about the number nine disturb her? Hoping to ease the ache gripping her head and neck, Erica dug three aspirin from her purse then grabbed a bottle of water and washed the pills down.

Juror Three, who occupied the chair to Erica's right, faced the foreman and raised her hand. "I apologize for interrupting the debate, but we ladies need a comfort break."

The burly man's narrowed eyes and clenched jaw spoke volumes.

"Trust me." The feisty middle-aged woman who'd dared disrupt the foreman scoffed as she pushed her chair away from the table. "Full bladders seriously diminish the mind's ability to focus on facts and come to any sort of logical conclusions."

"I'll give you exactly ten minutes." The foreman's tone made it clear he considered the disruption more than mildly annoying.

Juror Number Three nudged Erica then headed straight to the exit. Grateful for the break, Erica rushed to the door, followed by the three remaining females. Outside the jury room, the bailiff lifted off his chair. "Follow me." He led them down the hall to the ladies room.

Three's head tilted. "How'd you know?"

He grinned. "Twenty-two years of experience, ma'am."

Desperate for a moment alone, Erica rushed inside, slipped into a stall, and locked the door. The walls seemed to close around her as she filled her lungs then slowly released the breath. She squeezed her eyes shut. A minute passed as she struggled to find answers. Why had the memory suddenly surfaced, and why did it refuse to slither back into its hiding place?

"Two more minutes." A tap on the door startled her eyes open.

"Are you all right?" Juror Three's voice hinted of concern.

Erica blinked. "I'm fine." Had she come across as convincing? The moment she vacated the stall, another juror brushed past her and pulled the door closed. Desperate to control her emotions and at least appear in control, Erica eased to the sink and pumped soap onto her hands.

Juror Three sidled beside her. "Is this your first trial?"

"As a juror yes, but not as a witness or as an observer." Erica rinsed away the soap then held her hands beneath the automatic air dryer.

"This is my third time to serve on a jury." Three leaned back against the sink. "The previous two were a cake walk compared to this one."

Juror Seven exited a stall. "If I'd had the slightest inkling about this case, I would have found some way to convince the lawyers to exclude me."

"That makes two of us." Erica pulled her hands away from the dryer.

"You can also add my name to that list." Three lathered her hands. "Especially since our foreman's head will likely explode if we're not back in our seats a second before ten minutes turn into eleven."

"He reminds me of my ex-husband." Juror Ten leaned close to the mirror, applied lipstick, then dabbed the corners of her mouth. "That man's boxers are perpetually in a wad."

"Hmm." Number Seven tapped her finger on her chin. "Do you suppose our foreman is a boxer or a brief sort of guy?"

"There's an all-important third option." Ten spun away from the mirror. "Does he go commando?"

Juror Five burst out laughing. "You've put a whole new spin on our foreman's persona."

"You all can blame me if the five of us fail to maintain composure the next time he quirks a brow and begins a sentence with 'in my experience.'"

Thankful for the comic relief, Erica managed a half smile. "Maybe we should ask for a vote to find out where we stand."

"Tell you what." Three nudged Erica's arm. "I'll make the request if you second my motion."

"Done."

She high-fived Erica. "We walked out with full bladders and are returning with a plan, which should prove the value of bathroom breaks."

Responding to a knock, Juror Ten yanked the door open. "Let me guess, our foreman is missing the fab five."

The bailiff snickered. "He's a piece of work, all right. At the same time, his type tends to keep the other eleven from steering too far off course."

Juror Three scoffed. "While driving them crazy in the process."

Thirteen minutes after escaping, they followed the bailiff back to the deliberation room. The foreman drummed his fingers on the table when the women returned to their seats. Ten pulled her chair close to the table. "Based on our discussions thus far, I suggest you conduct a straw poll to determine how close we are to a decision."

Erica raised her hand. "I second the motion."

The foreman's fingers stopped drumming. "I'm way ahead of you." He distributed small sheets of paper listing three options. After everyone marked their ballot, Mr. What Type of Underwear Does He Prefer divided the votes into three piles. "Three guilty. Four not guilty. Five undecided. We still have a long way to go." He tossed the ballots in the trash, then crossed his arms on the table. His lip curled into a smirk. "To reiterate the facts, Summer Finch is accused of attempted homicide—"

"You're forgetting the most important fact." Juror Ten snapped her fingers. "The defendant's drunken stepfather fell backward and hit his neck on the corner of her dresser."

Number Eight sneered. "Only after she slammed a book upside his head and doomed him to life in a wheelchair."

Erica winced. "At least now he's no longer able to follow through on his threats or actions."

"We're dealing with the defendant's word against his."

Ten glared at the man sporting a full beard. "Assuming Summer is telling the truth, how many times should she have allowed her stepfather to molest her before defending herself? Once? Twice? A dozen?"

The bearded juror's eyes narrowed. "Her own mother believes her daughter overreacted."

Seven scoffed. "Because her mother can't bring herself to admit she'd brought a predator into their home." The woman jabbed her finger toward an array of photographs tacked to a board. "How do you explain the defendant's closest friend's testimony about those text messages or all the pictures of bruises Summer sent her following the two previous times she'd fought off the creep?"

Juror Eight shrugged. "She's a teenager. Maybe she wanted attention."

"There's another question to consider." Eleven twisted the cap off his water bottle. "If she was afraid of her stepfather, why didn't she report the earlier incidents to the police?"

Erica bristled as the newly surfaced memory skittered through her head in vivid detail. "Because Summer was ashamed."

Juror Four gawked at Erica. "Are you suggesting she tempted her stepfather?"

Erica fought to remain calm. "What I'm trying to say is victims often blame themselves, especially when their loved ones don't believe them. In Summer's case, her mother is in total denial—"

"Or she knows her daughter exaggerates."

Erica faced Juror Four. "If anything, a teenage girl would understate an act of violence."

The foreman rapped his pen on the table. "Given we haven't broken free from the gridlock, I'll review everything we learned during the trial."

Relieved he hadn't preceded his statement with 'in my experience,' Erica leaned back and folded her hands on her lap. While the self-proclaimed leader rehashed dozens of key points and testimonies presented by the opposing sides, Erica's mind wandered to the three-room apartment she had shared with her mother and younger brother before he was killed in a drive-by shooting. The tattered furniture. The dirty dishes piled in the sink. The stale odor of fried food and cigarette smoke. The memory she had blocked out.

Moments after the foreman's monologue finally ended, the debate resumed. Following two more hours of jurors digging in and defending their positions, the foreman initiated another vote. "Three guilty. Seven not guilty. Two undecided. At least we've made progress."

Juror Seven heaved a sigh. "I don't know about the rest of you, but my brain is suffering from information overload."

"I'm right there with you." Juror One cleared his throat. "Who votes we call it a night and pick back up tomorrow?" Every juror except one raised their hand.

"All right." Mr. Is He Boxer, Brief, or Commando's jaw clenched. "We'll reconvene at seven-thirty a.m. sharp. Don't forget the judge's order not to discuss the trial with anyone outside this room." After notifying the bailiff they were leaving for the night, he stood at the door as the jurors exited.

Cool evening air nipped Erica's cheeks while she made her way across West Main to Abby's car. Streetlights cast a warm glow on the park and downtown. Why had the memory from all those years ago escaped its hiding place two weeks before Valentine's Day? Was it some sort of sign about her relationship with Brad? She slid onto the driver's seat, clutched the steering wheel, and checked the rear-view mirror, noting her furrowed brows. What was the significance of the number nine?

Chapter 3

After five mornings of Millie's bout with a debilitating cold, Amanda tiptoed from her bedroom and crept down the dark hall. She stopped beside the guest room and leaned close. All seemed quiet behind the closed door. Hopefully the work crews would have their houseguest's fire-damaged home move-in ready before Valentine's Day. Amanda had to admit she'd grown accustomed to having their cranky neighbor as a houseguest, especially those nights Millie cooked dinner.

Amanda inched away from the door then breathed in the rich coffee aroma and ambled toward light spilling from the den. Erica curled up in a club chair beside the den fireplace cradling her favorite mug. "How long have you been awake?"

"A little more than an hour." Erica puffed her cheeks and released a long sigh. "With Millie out sick, jury duty couldn't have come at a more inconvenient time."

"At least the rest of our household has been spared her germs. Besides, Bernie and I are managing Hilltop's breakfast experience like champs. You'd be amazed at how much she's learned since you hired her as our housekeeper and morning assistant." Amanda moved closer to Erica and lowered her voice. "Would you believe Bernie's cinnamon buns are almost as delicious as our chef's?"

"If Millie finds out, she'll have a conniption."

"Which is why I won't breathe a word to another living soul. Although since Bernie is now our backup chef, I compliment her like crazy."

"Smart move. Especially since chocolate-chip pancakes are my one and only breakfast specialty."

Amanda snapped her fingers. "Good idea for tomorrow's menu." She headed to their galley-style kitchen. After preparing her own caffeine jolt, she returned to the den and settled on the matching club chair. "What are the chances your jury will deliver a verdict today?"

Erica stared at the fireplace as if expecting the flickering flame to provide the answer. "The facts in this case aren't as obvious as the evidence was in the murder charge against Gunter."

"Fingerprints on the murder weapon were indisputable." Amanda hesitated. Should she ask questions about today's trial or wait for Erica to volunteer information? Curiosity won out. "Are you dealing with a murder charge?"

"Attempted homicide."

"Is the defendant a man or a woman?"

Erica shook her head. "A teenaged girl. You know I can't tell you any more until the trial is over."

"I hope every juror is as diligent about not discussing the details as you are."

"Even though our foreman is as irritating as an incurable itch, at least he's a stickler for following the rules."

Abby maneuvered her wheelchair around the corner and into the den. Dusty, her golden retriever, padded beside her. "How's the trial going, Mom?"

Erica shrugged. "If today turns out anything like yesterday, we'll still be arguing next week."

"Here's hoping that isn't the case." After Abby opened the sliding glass door to let Dusty out to the backyard, she wheeled into the kitchen, followed by Erica.

Following the neurologist's instructions to let Abby do things by herself, Erica refilled her mug while her daughter removed a carton of orange juice and a tub of butter from the fridge. Why was her child's healing process moving at a snail's pace? Shouldn't she be walking by now? "What time is Tommy driving you to the Crisis Center this morning?"

"He's picking us up at seven."

"Us?"

"I'm taking Dusty with me today to comfort two new little kids who came in with their mother late yesterday." Abby removed the twist tie off a package of bread. "I suggested adopting an emotional support dog to stay at the center twenty-four seven."

"What a great idea."

"The board will vote on the proposal next week. Do you want some toast?"

"No thanks. I ate a little while ago."

Abby dropped two slices into the toaster. "Is Mr. Barkley taking you someplace special for Valentine's Day?"

"I don't know." The memory unleashed during the trial loomed large and refused to slither back into Erica's subconscious. At what point should she confide in Brad?

"After work, Tommy and I will bring Dusty back here then go to dinner and a movie."

"Sounds like fun." With Abby away for the evening and Millie recuperating in the guest room, maybe tonight would be the perfect time to share the memory with Amanda. Erica glanced at her watch. "I need to finish getting ready to leave." She leaned down and kissed her daughter's cheek. "Have a great day, sweetheart."

"Thanks, Mom. You too."

Forty minutes later, Erica found a parking spot a block from the courthouse. She stepped out of Abby's car, pulled her fur collar tight around her neck, and rushed to the courthouse steps. After entering the lobby and passing through security behind two jurors, she collected her belongings.

Juror Five waited for her. "I hope we arrive at a consensus before the end of the day. Especially since tomorrow is Saturday."

"You and me both."

The woman nodded toward Juror Eight. "Based on his comment about the defendant's word against her accuser, I suspect he's one of the guilty verdicts."

"Maybe he's had a change of heart since yesterday." The closer they came to the jury room, the faster Erica's pulse raced. During the past year she had helped settle plenty of disagreements among her partners. Dealing with conflict among eleven strangers who held a young woman's future in their hands was another story.

When Erica and Juror Five arrived at their destination, the bailiff greeted them with a smile. "Morning, ladies. Hot coffee and donuts are waiting for you."

"Thanks." Inside the deliberation room, Erica grabbed a bottle of water off a side table then settled on the seat she had vacated yesterday.

Sitting beside her, Juror Three swallowed a bite then wiped her fingers with a napkin. "The donuts are delicious. You should try one."

"Maybe later."

The last two jurors entered and settled in their places, prompting the foreman to pull his chair close to the table. "Now that everyone has had time to rest, let's find out where we stand." He distributed ballots. After the jurors cast their votes, he read each aloud and placed them in two piles. "Nine not guilty. Two guilty. One undecided." Mr. Brief, Boxer, or Commando leaned back, crossed his arms, and scanned the room. "Given we're three votes from a verdict, it's time to hear the holdouts' opinions. Let's begin with our undecided juror."

Silence.

"I'm not afraid to speak up." Juror Eight crossed his forearms on the table. "In my opinion, the defendant is guilty because there isn't a shred of forensic evidence proving her stepfather intended to molest her."

Juror Three faced the skeptical man. "Why else would a middle-aged man go into a teenaged girl's bedroom after she'd turned in for the night?"

"Maybe he just want to kiss her goodnight."

Juror Three tilted her head. "Remember he was drunk."

"Yeah, so what? Maybe he entered her room by mistake."

Ten minutes into the resulting debate, it became clear Juror Eleven was the other guilty vote. Undecided remained anonymous.

"Given we're at an impasse—" The foreman unfolded his arms and leaned forward. "I'll review the evidence and testimonies again."

Sighs and grumbles abounded.

Their foreman drummed his fingers. "If any one of you has a better idea, speak up."

No one uttered a word.

"Exactly what I thought." For three painfully long hours, their foreman ticked off details amid questions and comments. When he finished, Juror Number One raised his hand. "I'm changing my vote from undecided to not guilty."

"Which leaves us with two guilty votes."

"Actually—" Twelve cleared his throat. "I'm moving from the dark side and casting my vote for not guilty."

The remaining holdout's jaw clenched, making it clear he hadn't budged.

As the jurors continued their verbal assaults, Erica studied Juror Eight's rigid body posture. Was something other than the trial preventing him from changing his position?

The foreman slammed his fist on the table. "A hung jury is not acceptable. What a waste of the taxpayers' money."

No one uttered a word, but the air was thick with tension.

Hoping to summon enough courage to assume the role of peacemaker, Erica sent up a silent prayer. Within moments the tightness gripping her shoulders vanished. "If I may share an observation—"

"We need facts, not opinions." The foreman's tone mocked as it did whenever a female juror spoke up.

Juror Ten waggled her finger at their self-appointed leader. "Chill already and let her speak."

The foreman's lips curled into a snarl. "You have two minutes."

Here goes. "The fact is, I was married to a police officer who used me as his punching bag." Erica paused to allow her comment to resonate. "Living with an abusive man is why I understand the defendant's self-defense reaction to her stepfather's threatened assault." She caught Juror Eight's eye. "Our perspectives about this case are shaped by our life experiences. If we knew what those are for you, we'd understand why you're reluctant to find Summer not guilty."

His eyes narrowed. "You wanna know why I'm reluctant to let her off the hook? I'll tell you why." His tone screamed of anger. "Two years ago a woman accused my brother of sexually harassing her at work. Their boss—a woman—fired him on the spot. His reputation in that town was damaged beyond repair. No one would hire him. His fiancée broke off their engagement. Ten months later his accuser admitted she had reacted out of anger over him rejecting her romantic advances." The juror's nostrils flared. "My brother was an innocent man who lost everything because one vindictive woman couldn't face rejection."

"Thank you for helping us see this case through your eyes." Erica leaned toward the juror. "During the last few days, I've had the opportunity to assess this case from a different, yet similar perspective."

Juror Eight's eyes narrowed to a slit. "Meaning what?"

"The same way your brother rejected the vindictive woman's advances, Summer refused to become her stepfather's victim. Instead of accepting responsibility for his actions, he's threatening to take everything away from Summer by falsely accusing her of attacking him without provocation. Today, we have the opportunity to do for this young woman what people failed to do for your brother."

No one moved until Juror Two raised his hand. "I suggest we take another vote."

"No need." The holdout's eyes remained trained on Erica. "I'm changing my position to not guilty."

A collective sigh resonated.

"All right, then." The foreman cleared his throat. "I'll tell the bailiff we've made a decision."

While the jurors heaped praise on the juror who had ended the deadlock, the woman sitting beside Erica leaned close. "Brilliant closing argument. If you're called to jury duty in the future, you should step up as forewoman."

"Thanks for the compliment, but without divine guidance, I would never have summoned enough courage to speak up."

Juror Three patted Erica's arm. "Whatever it takes to arrive at the truth, honey."

The jurors enjoyed a tension-free lunch and chatted about their favorite teams in the upcoming Super Bowl and favorite restaurants while waiting for the judge to call them back into the courtroom. At five minutes before two, the bailiff stepped into the jury room. "We're ready for you."

The twelve lined up and filed into the jury box. The stepfather's chin jutted as he turned toward the jurors. Would the verdict shock or anger him?

The judge faced the jury box. "Have you reached a verdict?"

Their foreman stood. "We have, Your Honor."

The bailiff carried the paper to the bench. After the judge read the decision, the bailiff returned it to the foreman.

The judge leaned forward. "How do you find in the case of the state of Georgia versus Summer Finch?"

Their foreman's shoulders squared. "We find Summer Finch..." He paused and appeared to eye the defendant. "Not guilty."

Summer broke down in tears. Her accuser released a string of expletives before wheeling his chair away from his attorney and out of the courtroom. Summer's mother rushed to embrace her daughter.

The judge faced the jury. "Thank you, ladies and gentlemen, for your service. You're excused."

As the jurors headed back to the jury room to collect their belongings, Eight pulled Erica aside. "I appreciate you helping me realize that my anger kept me from recognizing the truth."

"We all have memories that cloud our judgement. Which is why it takes twelve jurors to reach a verdict."

"Thanks to you, we won't be forced to spend our weekend arguing this case."

Erica nodded. "In the end, we all came together as a team." Seven hours after entering the courthouse, Erica walked out to the bright sunshine and dug her sunglasses from her purse. Relieved the temperature had risen to a comfortable level, she shielded her eyes from the sun's glare then descended the front stairs to the sidewalk. Hoping a few minutes alone would clear her mind, she strolled two blocks then turned right at Depot Street.

Erica paused beside the blue train engine sitting idle on the track until the tourist season picked back up. Thankfully, Hilltop maintained a seventy percent occupancy rate after the winter train rides to McCaysville ended, providing proof their marketing strategies paid off. Erica smiled at a couple passing by while resuming her stroll. At the intersection she waited for the light to change then crossed the street to the sidewalk fronting the East Main Street shops.

The temperature had been frigid the day she'd first met Amanda and Wendy in Blue Ridge Inn's dining room and agreed to a shopping spree. Even though heavy snow had been forecasted that day more than a year ago, Amanda had purchased a hooded sweatshirt. Funny how she had claimed buying a coat she would only wear a few times was a waste of money. At least now Awesam's president owned a proper winter coat.

Three teenaged girls wearing sweatshirts walked out of Sweet Shoppe munching on cookies and passed by her. Two doors down she stopped in front of Owl's Nest and eyed the window display. During their first shopping spree, she and her new friends didn't have a clue they'd end up selling most of their possessions and all their jewelry to pay the back taxes and transform the Harrington estate into an inn. Now a year later, Hilltop and her massage therapy business finally provided a decent living, so she could afford to splurge a bit. Especially today. Erica lifted her chin and stepped inside.

Jennifer, the owner, who had become a good friend, greeted her with a smile. "Two of Hilltop's guests left a few minutes ago."

"I hope they spent a lot of money."

"Their visit was successful for both of us." Jennifer looped her arm around Erica's elbow. "Are you shopping for something special or just browsing?"

"Actually, I need to replace some of the jewelry I sold before moving to Blue Ridge."

"We'll help you find whatever you need." Jennifer motioned to one of her assistants. "Take good care of our friend."

How gracious the residents always were, welcoming the Awesam partners into their close-knit community. Erica followed the young woman to a glass case.

"I love your necklace."

Erica touched the diamond heart suspended inches below her neck. How many people were aware she and Brad had been dating? "A Christmas gift from a special friend."

"Our high school principal, Mr. Barkley?"

Apparently a lot of people had seen her and Brad together. One more reality of small-town life. "Yes."

"Everyone loves him, especially his students. He was the best football coach our town ever had."

"So, I've heard."

"He also has great taste in jewelry. If you're looking for something to complement your necklace, check these out." The assistant moved a display showcasing an array of sparkly earrings close to Erica.

After viewing dozens of options, Erica carried three pairs of earrings and one bracelet to the checkout counter. While Jennifer packaged her purchases, they chatted about the inn and her new sister store, Bungalow Bleu.

The moment another customer stepped up, Erica bid her friend goodbye, then returned to the sidewalk and headed back toward the courthouse.

Two doors down Erica halted in front of Sweet Shoppe. Should she indulge? Definitely yes, especially after enduring a difficult trial. Mouthwatering aromas greeted her the moment when she stepped inside and waited her turn. Ten minutes after first peering into the glass display case, she walked out carrying a box of assorted cupcakes.

By the time Erica pulled into the ranch house carport, she had summoned the courage to share her past with one of her two Victory Sorority Sisters. The new name brought a smile to her face. She, Amanda, and Wendy had chosen it to replace 'Exclusive Wives Club'. Little did Gunter Benson know his deceptions had created a unique family who had refused to become victims and turned tragedy into triumph.

Bolstered by self-confidence, Erica strode into the kitchen. She dropped her keys, purse, and Owl's Nest bag on the counter, then walked into the den and placed the Sweet Shoppe box on the dining room table.

Amanda looked up from her laptop. "A treat to celebrate victory?"

"A not guilty verdict." Erica sat across from Awesam's president. Dusty padded over and sprawled at her feet. "Now I can talk about the trial."

"I'm all ears." Amanda pushed her laptop aside.

Erica spent an hour sharing details and answering questions. When she finished relaying the conversation with Juror Number Eight that led to the verdict, Amanda applauded. "Well done, Ms. CEO Slash Peacemaker. Is it time to celebrate with a Sweet Shoppe indulgence?"

"Not yet. There's something else I need to talk to you about." Erica pulled in a deep breath. "A troubling memory from my past surfaced during the trial."

"What sort of memory?" Millie sauntered in and plopped onto a chair.

Erica stared wide eyed at the interloper. How could she have heard from the guest room?

Amanda faced Hilltop's chef. "Well, look who's come out of hibernation."

"Ready to catch up on all the news." Millie faced Erica. "Go ahead."

Erica avoided eye contact. "It's not important." Did she sound convincing?

"Are you serious?" Millie's body appeared to collapse in on itself. "Not only am I Awesam's chief information officer, but I've also been living in your house for months. And you still don't trust me?"

"It's not that I don't trust you—"

"What other reason could you possibly have for clamming up the second I walked into the room?"

Erica's cheeks burned. How would she feel if the situation were reversed? Humiliated.

Amanda touched their chef's arm. "Look—"

"You don't need to intervene on my behalf, Amanda. Millie's right. She's proven her loyalty and discretion."

"Thank you." Millie's shoulders lifted. "Now, what images did the trial release from your memory file?"

Erica breathed deeply then slowly released the air. "My brother, mother, and I lived in a three-room, walk-up apartment in one of the poorest Baltimore neighborhoods."

Millie's brow pinched. "Where was your father?"

"I have no idea. Mom never talked about him. Anyway, there was this one day…" As the incident which had remained hidden for decades poured out, a single question loomed large. How much of the memory should she share with Brad?

Chapter 4

Light spilling from the lamp on the other side of the king-size bed nudged Wendy awake. A smile curled her lips the moment her eyes focused on the new cowgirl hat she'd sent flying across the room last night. She rolled toward her soulmate.

Chris pulled her into his arms. "Good morning, Angel."

Wendy breathed in the lingering scent of his cologne. "How long have you been awake?"

"Couple of minutes."

Their baby's babble emanated from across the room.

"Our little guy's awake and happy." Chris kissed Wendy's cheek then climbed out of bed and ambled to the crib tucked against the wall beside the desk. He lifted his son into his arms. "Are you ready for a fun Saturday exploring Music City?" He blew a raspberry on Ryan's neck triggering a full-belly laugh. "I'll take your response as a yes."

Wendy's heart danced with joy as she plucked her robe off the floor and headed to the bathroom. She turned on the shower and waited for steam to fog the mirror then stepped into the enclosure. Warm water cascading over her body summoned delicious images from last night's private party for two. Wendy pressed her hand to her chest and thanked God for bringing Chris into her life then hummed a favorite tune while luxuriating in the shower.

After stepping out of the enclosure and drying her hair, Wendy donned her robe and returned to the bedroom. Sitting between Chris's legs on the bed, Ryan plucked a piece of banana off the tray and stuffed it into his mouth. Wendy unplugged her phone from the charger and snapped a picture. "Another memory of our first family vacation. After your daddy showers, we'll go back to Cascades for breakfast." The moment Chris scooted off the bed, Wendy sat beside her little guy and pinched off another piece of banana. "You have the best daddy in the world." One day when Ryan was old enough to understand, they would tell him his daddy loved him so much he legally adopted him as his own.

Following a leisurely breakfast and a stroll through the atrium, they made their way to the hotel entrance. A valet pulled their car under the veranda. Grateful for the cloudless sky and fifty-five-degree weather, Wendy buckled Ryan into his car seat while Chris stowed his stroller in the trunk. They drove away from the property, Wendy humming along to a tune playing on the radio.

Chris chuckled. "When did you become a country music fan?"

"Hmm." Wendy ran her fingers along her new hat rim. "When I married the smartest attorney in Georgia and discovered how much he enjoys southern gals who wear fancy cowgirl hats."

Chris winked. "Just one gorgeous southern gal, mind you."

During the ride to their destination, Wendy continued humming while imagining caring for two babies. "Would you prefer our second child be a boy or a girl?"

"Definitely one or the other."

"I'm leaning toward a girl." Wendy giggled at Ryan's demonstrative babble. "Our little guy obviously has an opinion. Too bad we don't have a clue what he's saying."

"One of these days he'll say something understandable."

"Based on his sounds, I'm guessing his first word will be dada." Wendy grinned and thumped Chris's arm. "Especially since you've been coaching him."

"You noticed?"

"Oh, yeah." Wendy peered out the passenger window when Chris pulled in front of the Gilmores' two-story brick house for the second time in two days. "I hope Kayla's right about no one other than her being home." As if on cue, her sister—wearing her new cowgirl hat—rushed out the front door then raced across the yard and climbed into the back seat beside her nephew. Wendy twisted toward the back the moment Ryan blew a bubble-drenched raspberry. "Our little guy's happy to see you."

"Hey, neph." Kayla buckled her belt. "I'm gonna take you and your mommy and daddy someplace special."

Chris glanced over his shoulder. "Where is this mystery destination?"

"Downtown." Kayla rattled off an address while Chris entered the location into his navigation App. She talked a blue streak about the Nashville music scene until Chris turned the corner a block from the address. "Pull into that parking garage. We'll walk from there." The moment they parked, Kayla unbuckled her belt and leaned forward. "I need to tell you something about where we're going." Her tone hinted of anxiety.

Chris chuckled. "You're not taking us some place illegal, are you?"

"Hardly. We're going to lunch...at Gilmore's."

Wendy pivoted to face her sister. "That name isn't a coincidence, is it?"

Kayla shook her head. "Even though I'm not gonna tell my dad we're related, I want you to meet him."

Chris stared at her. "How exactly do you intend to explain who we are?"

"No brainer. Wendy's my friend."

"What if your father asks how you two met?"

Kayla shrugged. "The same way all kids connect. Social media."

"Lying is never a good idea."

Kayla stared at Chris as if he didn't have a clue. "He's lying about Mom's health, so why should I worry about telling the truth?"

Wendy's heart ached for her sister. "Not telling you what's wrong with your mother isn't the same as lying."

Kayla rolled her eyes. "Whatever." She climbed out making it clear there was nothing more to discuss.

Chris locked eyes with Wendy. "I'm not wild about this."

"Believe me, I understand. At the same time, I doubt Mr. Gilmore will ever find out who we really are, so what's the harm?"

"Do you want me to list all the reasons your sister's idea is nuts?"

Wendy trilled her lips. "Not really."

Kayla rapped on the passenger window. "What are you guys waiting for?"

Wendy's eyes remained trained on Chris. "Meeting her father is obviously important to her."

"Only because this is important to you." He unbuckled his seatbelt. "Against my better judgement, we'll go."

Wendy stretched across the console and kissed his cheek. "Thank you, darling."

"You won't thank me if this meeting goes off the rails."

"It won't."

"I hope you're right."

Wendy climbed out, opened the back door, and released Ryan from his seat. After securing him in his stroller, they made their way through the parking garage. Once they reached the pedestrian-filled sidewalk, Wendy donned her sunglasses. How was she going to handle meeting the man her mother had abandoned her for all those years ago? The man who didn't have a clue about his wife's secret child. Or did he? When they crossed the street and headed up the block, doubt began to creep in. Wendy's pulse accelerated the moment the restaurant came into view. Maybe she should have listened to Chris. Especially since fifteen-year-olds weren't known for making the best decisions.

Kayla rushed ahead to the corner.

Chris slowed his pace. "There's still time to back out."

"I don't want to disappoint her. Besides, she's already holding the door open for us."

When they caught up with Kayla, her face beamed. "Welcome to Gilmore's Bar and Grill."

Wendy took measured breaths to slow her racing heart. She stepped inside, Chris following with the stroller. Country music mingling with lively chatter created a casual atmosphere. Customers relaxed on barstools and gathered around tables on two sides of a raised stage. Somehow the baby grand piano seemed out of place beside drums and guitars. "Who plays the piano?"

"Dad, except when Mom sings with the band, then she plays. I also play. Dad taught both of us."

A hostess clad in western attire greeted them with a smile. "Hey, girl. Are you here to talk to your dad or enjoy lunch with your friends?"

"A little of both."

"You know he's always happy when you drop by. I'll take care of the stroller for you folks."

"Thanks." Chris lifted Ryan into his arms while Wendy plucked the diaper bag from the back.

"Come with me, folks." The hostess led them to a table beside the stage. "I'll bring a high chair for your baby."

Wendy sat with her back to the bar and peered at photos and record albums tastefully displayed on the brick walls surrounding the window facing the street. Kayla settled across from her. "Does your dad's band play every day?"

"Six nights a week from eight until midnight. A couple times a month Mom sings with them. Guest bands play every day starting at five."

The hostess returned and placed the high chair between Wendy and Chris. "What's your baby's name?"

"Ryan."

"He's adorable, and he looks a lot like his handsome daddy."

The first few times strangers had offered the same comment, Wendy hadn't known how to react. Until she realized Ryan could easily pass as Chris's flesh and blood. "It's obvious who's our little guy's daddy."

The hostess placed menus on the table. "I'll let Mr. Gilmore know you're here."

After Chris placed Ryan in the high chair, Wendy swiped a baby wipe across the tray, then placed bits of cereal on the clean surface. "Is this a popular destination for tourists or for locals?"

"Both." Kayla's chest puffed. "Gilmore's is one of the best bars with the best live band in Nashville."

Wendy smiled at her sister. "You're proud of your father, aren't you?"

She nodded. "Dad is a great singer, as good as a lot of famous country stars."

A good-looking, middle-aged man wearing cowboy boots, jeans, and a plaid shirt approached. "What a nice surprise."

"Hey, Dad. Meet my friends Wendy and Chris Armstrong and their son Ryan."

He extended his hand to Wendy. "Brent Gilmore."

"It's a pleasure."

"Likewise." After shaking Chris's hand, he sat across from him then eyed Wendy. "You're the first married couple Kayla has brought to our family business. How do you know my daughter?"

Wendy's shoulders stiffened. Had he noticed how much she favored his wife?

"Really, Dad?" Kayla rolled her eyes. "Do you have any idea how many social media friends I've actually met in person?"

"Now I know at least two."

"Dad has written songs for five different singers. Four of them were big hits."

Brent fingered his neatly trimmed beard. "Those royalties provided the funds to buy this place. Are you country music fans?"

"I am now, thanks to my husband." Hoping to prevent any awkward moments, Wendy leaned forward. "Do you still write music?"

"Yes, but exclusively for my band. What do you folks do for a living?"

Chris folded his arms on the table. "I'm an attorney and my wife's a chief financial officer."

"Here in Nashville?"

"In Blue Ridge, Georgia. Wendy and I are on a much-needed vacation."

"You picked the perfect town for a little R and R." Brent motioned a waitress over. "Take good care of these folks and put their meal on my tab."

"Yes, sir."

After ordering, Chris steered the conversation to Nashville tourist sites and football. When their food arrived, Kayla's father stood. "I'll leave you folks to enjoy lunch. The next time you're in Nashville, come by after dark so you can hear us play." He bent down and kissed his daughter's cheek. "Thanks for introducing me to your friends, honey."

"You're welcome. See you later, Dad."

Wendy's eyes followed Brent Gilmore as he strode to the bar and stopped to chat with customers. Had Kayla insisted they meet her father because he was a good guy, or did she have some sort of ulterior motive? Wendy's focus shifted to the piano then to her half-sister. "When will I have the opportunity to hear you play?"

"The next time you come to Nashville."

"Promise?"

Kayla shrugged. "Sure, why not."

Chapter 5

After changing clothes twice, Erica settled on black pants and a red sweater. At least she'd look cheery. She dropped onto her bedroom chair, balanced her laptop on her thighs, and opened Hilltop's reservation tab. Two massages scheduled for Monday, none for tomorrow. How many appointments had jury duty cost her?

Erica logged off and set her laptop on the bed. Brad would pull into their driveway in ten minutes. Amanda and Millie had both encouraged her to share the decades-old memory with him. In her heart she believed they were right, but to what end?

How many hours had she spent alone in this room sorting through her emotions? The room that had become her private space in the house she shared with strangers who had become her extended family. She ran her fingers across the dresser she had brought from one of her Asheville guestrooms. Thankfully, she had kept enough furniture to create a comfortable living space.

Erica spritzed perfume behind her ears then lifted her coat off the bed and headed to the den. Amanda lounged on a club chair reading a book while Millie tackled a crossword puzzle at the dining room table—her partners' go-to activities to keep the peace.

Millie looked up. "Any news on Abby's latest CAT scan?"

Erica shook her head. "We'll learn the results during Thursday's appointment with her neurologist."

"Red is a good color to wear on a date." Millie leaned back. "What time do you expect Brad to bring you home?"

Amanda scoffed. "There you go playing the role of housemother again."

Millie waggled her finger. "Don't tell me you're not curious about tonight's outcome."

"Even though Erica shared her memory with us, what happens between her and Brad tonight is their business."

Would their quibbling ever end? "I have no idea what time I'll come home, so relax and try to get along."

"Good idea. Especially since it's just the two of us." Millie pushed her chair away from the table. "How about I make us a couple of Monte Cristo sandwiches? Then we can watch a movie."

"Beats the heck out of arguing." Amanda closed her book. "Especially if we add a couple glasses of wine to the plan."

Millie snapped her fingers. "Now you're talking. Red or white?"

"Red." Amanda laid her book on the end table. "I'll do the honors."

Grateful to hear the front doorbell, Erica donned her coat and headed toward the foyer.

Amanda flicked her a wave. "Enjoy your evening, and don't worry about Millie and me. We'll figure out how to get along for a few hours without you playing peacemaker."

"Good." Arctic air accosted Erica the moment she pulled the door open and stepped onto the porch. "Hi."

Brad leaned close. "You look beautiful." His warm breath caressed her cheek.

"Thank you." Erica pulled her fur collar tight around her neck.

Brad pressed his hand to her back while they hastened to his nineteen-year-old red Corvette. He opened the passenger door. After Erica slid onto the warm leather seat, he dashed to the driver's side and climbed in beside her.

Resisting the urge to run her fingers through his curly brown hair, she buckled her seatbelt. "Thank you for warming the seat for me."

His smile crinkled the skin around his blue eyes. "My pleasure." Brad pulled his seatbelt across his chest. "How's Abby's therapy going?"

Erica sighed. "Progress is slower than I had hoped. What's going on with Jimmy?"

"He's finally out of his cast. He'll need to use a cane until therapy strengthens his leg muscles." Brad backed down the driveway. "Yesterday Jimmy and Ashley drove to Atlanta."

"To live?"

Brad shook his head. "Her leave of absence ran out." He stopped at the corner then turned toward town. "Ashley's moving to Blue Ridge."

"To your house?"

"No. She rented a two-bedroom apartment close to downtown. Jimmy plans to move in with her."

"Is a wedding in their future?"

"They're taking one step at a time. There's a teaching position opening up for Ashley in a few months. Jimmy hasn't decided what he wants to do."

Erica ran her fingers along her seatbelt. Even though Abby's accident wasn't technically Jimmy's fault, he still struggled with guilt. Brad turned onto another road, making it clear where he was taking her. Would the destination strengthen or weaken her resolve? Her pulse accelerated as he pulled onto the driveway leading to his white single-story house with stone trim centered on a wooded lot.

Brad parked in his garage then escorted Erica to his front door for the second time since they had met at Hilltop Inn's grand opening party last spring. Soft background music and the succulent aroma of tomatoes, garlic, and rosemary greeted them the moment they stepped into the foyer.

"Lasagna?"

"Spaghetti."

"It smells delicious."

"My other Italian specialty."

Erica peered into the tastefully decorated contemporary living and dining room. An array of family photos still adorned the white brick fireplace mantel. Her eyes drifted to the prominently displayed photo of herself. Brad had snapped the casual picture from across the table during one of their restaurant dates.

"One of these days I'll add a picture of the two of us."

She blinked. Had her expression hinted that she'd noticed the picture?

"Ashley told me she mentioned the picture to you at Jimmy's trial."

"Oh."

After helping her slip out of her coat, Brad looped his hand around her elbow. He escorted Erica to the cozy kitchen featuring dark wood cabinets and marble countertops. A bottle of Barolo sat on the island beside two wine glasses. "We're going full Italian tonight." He uncorked the bottle, poured, and handed Erica a glass.

She sipped the dark red wine. "Delicious."

"Jan always wanted to visit Italy." Brad turned on the burner under a pasta pot. "The closest we came was watching *Roman Holiday*—one of her favorite old movies."

"I've never seen that film."

"An Audrey Hepburn, Gregory Peck black-and-white classic. Definitely a chick flick." Brad slid a loaf of garlic bread in the oven and set a timer.

Erica set her glass on the island and ran her finger around the rim. "What's your favorite movie?"

"A tossup between *Remember the Titans* and *We Are Marshall*. Both true football stories."

"Perfect choices for a former award-winning coach turned principal." Erica paused. "What about *Blind Side*?"

"Another good one." Brad stirred the sauce then dropped spaghetti noodles into boiling water and set a second timer. "Do you have a favorite movie?"

"*The Notebook* and *Bridges of Madison County* are two of my all-time favorites."

"Not exactly guy flicks, but then what guy wouldn't appreciate movies starring James Garner and Clint Eastwood? Even if they are romantic tearjerkers."

"Here's a question." Erica tilted her head. "From a man's perspective, in *Bridges* should Meryl Streep have followed her heart and run away with the photographer?"

"She did."

"Did what?"

"Follow her heart." Brad grinned. "Which is why she stayed with her family."

A football coach with a soft side. Should she share the memory with him now? Better to wait until after her second glass of wine. "Is there something I can do to help?"

"Sure." He removed a bowl of torn romaine, a bottle of dressing, and a package of shaved parmesan from the refrigerator, "Do you mind finishing the salad?"

"Glad to." They continued to talk about movies until the first timer dinged.

Brad removed the bread from the oven releasing olive oil and garlic scents. Erica prepared the salad while he drained and plated noodles. Helping prepare a meal in this kitchen with this man felt natural, even intimate, and yet—

"The Barkley version of an Italian dinner is served."

Erica set the salad bowls on the table then slid onto the padded banquette built into the bay window. Brad sat across from her and held her hand while blessing their meal. When he finished, he refilled their wine glasses. "Another little taste of Italy."

During dinner they talked about food, their jobs, and golf. Following their last bites of spaghetti, Brad carried their plates to the sink, then returned with two plates of tiramisu. Erica tasted. "Oh my gosh, this is delicious. Another testament to your culinary skills?"

"I wish I could take the credit, but no." After they finished the dessert, Brad leaned back, grinning. "There's no place I'd rather be than here with you."

How should she respond? "I always enjoy your company, especially when you prepare such delicious meals."

"I've been giving us a lot of thought, and well…" Brad pulled a black velvet box from his pocket.

Erica's heart jumped to her throat. Why of all nights had he chosen tonight?

He gazed deep into her eyes. "You're not ready, are you?"

Would he understand? "Something happened during the trial you need to know about." Erica pushed her plate aside. "A memory that has remained buried deep in my subconscious for years suddenly broke free."

Brad laid the box on the table. His eyes remained locked on hers. "I'm listening."

Erica breathed deeply to slow her racing pulse. "I was ten years old the day I came home from school and found two men carrying my mother strapped to a gurney down our building's front steps. When they loaded her into an ambulance, I didn't know if I'd ever see her again."

Brad reached for her hand and stroked her fingers with his thumb.

"Ms. Ginger, Mom's best friend—probably her only friend—held my hand as the ambulance sped away and disappeared around the corner. I asked her if my mother was dead. She said no, then led me inside and up to her apartment across the hall from ours. Unlike our place, her apartment smelled fresh like vanilla and lemons. Sunshine poured in through sparkly clean windows. We sat at her kitchen table while she explained how she had found my mother passed out on our kitchen floor." The memory sent a shudder ripping through Erica.

Brad squeezed her hand. "You don't have to finish—"

"I need to tell you everything." She took a sip of wine. "Ms. Ginger asked if I knew why my mother was an addict. I said because she drank too much and took pills she bought from a guy she met out on the street in front of our building. Ms. Ginger told me mother's addiction was the result, not the cause. I didn't understand what she meant."

Erica broke eye contact as another memory crystalized. "She poured me a glass of milk and set a plate of freshly baked cookies on the table. Then she explained that my mother, grandmother, and great-grandmother were uneducated women who had become the casualties of generational poverty. She told me they didn't have the will or self-discipline to stand on their own two feet. Instead all three allowed themselves to become victims of abusive and corrupt men. Ms. Ginger told me I was destined to end the cycle. She was wrong. After my brother was killed by a drive-by shooter, I married an abuser, then years later a con man."

Her eyes met Brad's. "I have fallen deeply in love with you." Erica fingered the heart necklace Brad had given her for Christmas. Would he understand what she needed? "However, for the first time in my life, I'm a successful, educated woman."

"So you want more time to excel on your own before committing to another marriage?"

Tears pooled and slid down Erica's cheeks. *He understood.* "Yes."

Brad lifted off his chair then slid onto the banquette beside her and wrapped his arm around her shoulders. "I want to spend the rest of my life loving and caring for you."

Erica faced him. "I'm sorry—"

Brad's gaze softened as he pressed his finger to her lips. "I want you to take the box home and open it when the time is right for you. When I see the ring on your finger, I'll know you're ready."

"I promise one day before too long, I will marry you."

Brad wiped away her tears with a tenderness that reached in and touched Erica's soul. "I'll wait for as long as you need, my love. For now, what do you say we forget cleaning up the kitchen, enjoy another glass of wine, and watch a movie?"

She sniffled. "I can't think of a better way to spend the evening."

Brad handed her his handkerchief then held her hand as they strolled to the den. He opened a cabinet. "Your choice."

Erica bent down and scanned the array of DVDs. Which would be most appropriate? Her eyes landed on one of her favorites. She handed it to Brad.

"*When Harry Met Sally.* A romantic comedy. Great choice." After sliding the disc into the player, they settled on the sofa. Brad slid his arm around Erica's shoulders as the movie began.

Hours later he drove her home and walked her to her front porch. He pulled her into his arms and kissed her tenderly. "Sleep well, my love."

Erica kissed him then stroked his cheek. "Thank you for tonight."

He winked. "Until our next date."

Erica unlocked the door and stepped inside then ambled to the den. Amanda, wearing pajamas and fuzzy socks, was curled up on the sofa with a book open on her lap. Erica's brow pinched. "It's past midnight. Why are you still awake?"

"Uncontrollable curiosity." Awesam's president closed her book and set it on the end table. "Did you tell Brad?"

"During dessert."

"How did he respond?"

"He understood." Erica tucked her purse under her arm and settled beside her. Her eyes drifted to the flame flickering in the fireplace while her lips curled into an involuntary smile.

Amanda stretched her arm across the back of the sofa. "What aren't you telling me?" Her voice was barely above a whisper.

"Promise you won't breathe a word to anyone except Wendy?"

"Cross my heart."

Erica removed the ring box from her purse.

Amanda's eyes widened. "Oh my gosh, Brad proposed—"

"Not exactly."

"How can a man not exactly pop the question?"

Erica replayed the evening for her partner.

"Brad Barkley is one of the most amazing men on the planet." Amanda pressed one hand to her chest and pointed skyward with the other. "Right up there with my Preston."

"After Brad's first love passed on to eternity, he believed he would spend the rest of his life alone."

"Until he met you."

Erica nodded. "I believe one day you'll find your second soulmate."

"The chances of a forty-four-year-old widow finding love in a small North Georgia town are as remote as winning the lottery without buying a ticket."

"Brad was in his forties when we met."

"Dating is different for women my age."

Millie padded into the den, yawning.

Startled, Erica stashed the ring box in her purse, hoping Millie was too sleepy to notice. "Did we wake you?"

She shook her head. "My decades-old bladder. Did you share your dream with Brad?"

"Yes." *Good, she hadn't noticed.*

Millie propped her hip on the sofa arm. "Then what happened?"

"He's giving me as much time as I need." Erica clutched her purse and lifted off her chair. "I don't know about you two, but I need a few hours of sleep before breakfast duty and tomorrow afternoon's board meeting."

Amanda stood and turned off the fire. "I'm right behind you."

"So am I." Millie lifted off the sofa arm and padded out of the den.

Erica tiptoed to her room to avoid waking Abby. Inside her private space, she pushed the door closed and turned on the overhead light. She pulled the box from her purse and slid it into her bottom dresser drawer under her summer shirts where it would remain until she became the woman she was meant to be and the soulmate Brad deserved. After changing into flannel pajamas, she turned off the light and climbed into bed. As the events of the past few hours played in her mind, one unsettling question remained. Would she ever understand why the number nine haunted her?

Chapter 6

Amanda turned off her nightstand lamp and slid under the down comforter she had purchased the week she and her partners moved to Blue Ridge. The moment she closed her eyes, her mind drifted back to the stormy New Orleans afternoon that changed her life forever. Preston kissing her cheek before stepping out of their shotgun house and dashing to his car parked at the curb. Wondered why he was taking so long to run a simple errand. The shocking phone call. Rushing to the hospital. Holding his hand as he slipped into eternity. If a drunk driver had stolen her life instead of her husband's, she wouldn't want Preston to spend the rest of his life alone.

The mere thought of dating sent a shiver cascading through Amanda's limbs. If God wanted her to fall in love again, he would have to intervene on her behalf. Moments after rolling onto her side, she fell into a deep sleep until her alarm jolted her awake at five a.m.

Resisting the urge to press snooze, Amanda climbed out of bed and donned her robe. She would for sure need a nap between church and Awesam's two o'clock board meeting. After a quick trip to the bathroom, she followed the scent of freshly brewed coffee to the kitchen.

Millie filled a mug and stirred in sugar, then handed it to her.

"Thank you." Amanda sipped while keeping her eyes trained on Hilltop's chef. Was preparing her coffee an act of kindness or a prelude to a bribe?

Millie leaned back against the counter and crossed her arms. "What were you and Erica talking about before I joined you in the den last night?"

Definitely a bribe. Amanda shrugged. "The spaghetti dinner Brad prepared and the movie they watched."

Millie tapped her foot on the linoleum floor. "You know what I'm talking about."

Erica ambled into the kitchen. "Good morning."

Amanda aimed her thumb over her shoulder. "Why don't you ask her?"

"Ask me what?" Erica yawned while removing a mug from the cabinet.

"Amanda will explain while I begin preparing breakfast for our guests." Millie donned her coat and headed out to the carport.

Erica filled her mug. "She wants to know what I told you about my date with Brad, right?"

Amanda nodded. "At least she's predictable."

Erica stirred sugar and creamer into her coffee. "Other than her son and daughter-in-law, we're Millie's only family. Maybe I should share a few more details."

Amanda stared wide-eyed at Awesam's CEO. "Not about the ring!"

"Are you serious? If I revealed that bit of news, Millie would hound the dickens out of both of us until I opened the box."

"For a second I thought you'd suffered a lapse of judgement."

"Just a little compassion. We need to head over shortly. Do you want to shower first?"

Amanda shook her head. "I showered last night. We'll walk over together as soon as you're ready."

"I won't take long." Erica spun around and hastened through the den.

Twenty minutes later, bundled in jackets, they stepped out to the carport and into the breezy predawn morning. Amanda pulled her jacket tight across her chest. "Have you figured out how much to tell Millie?"

"I'm getting there."

They hastened to the inn's front sidewalk then climbed onto the covered porch and unlocked the front door. Inside, two elderly guests who had arrived the day before sipped coffee on the living room sofa.

Amanda summoned her best smile. "Good morning, Mr. and Mrs. Dixon. I hope you enjoyed a wonderful evening."

The woman turned in their direction. "We began with dinner at the General Ledger."

Mr. Dixon chuckled. "Today my wife is eager to support the local economy."

"There are so many wonderful places to shop." Erica brushed a dark strand of hair away from her face. "One of our favorites is Owl's Nest."

"If you're in the mood for the best cupcakes in the south, check out the Sweet Shoppe," added Amanda.

Mr. Dixon grinned. "I'll indulge while my wife shops."

"My husband is crazy about sweets."

He patted his wife's knee. "One of the many reasons I fell in love with you sixty-two years ago, my dear."

She kissed his cheek.

Erica grinned. "You're a delightful couple."

"Before you head to town, you'll enjoy a delicious breakfast." Amanda slipped out of her jacket. "Our award-winning chef serves the best cinnamon buns—her own special recipe." After a glance at the list of today's checkouts, Amanda followed Erica to the kitchen. "What's on the menu?"

"Cheddar and bacon quiche and home fries." Millie spread icing onto warm cinnamon buns. "Yogurt's ready to serve."

"I'm on it." Amanda removed a bowl from the fridge and began filling fruit cups.

Erica hung her jacket over the back of a stool then lined up twelve plates on the island. "To answer your question to Amanda earlier, I shared my childhood memory with Brad last night. He's okay with me needing more time."

"He obviously believes you're worth waiting for." Millie aimed her spatula at Amanda. "Erica trusts me, so why don't you?"

"It's not a matter of trust—"

"Then why wouldn't you tell me?"

"I've told you before and now I'll tell you again. When you want to know something about Erica or Wendy or anyone else in our family, ask them, not me."

"I suppose I shouldn't put you in awkward positions."

Amanda gawked at Millie. "Finally, you understand."

She scoffed. "You don't need to get all huffy."

"In case you've both forgotten—" Erica stepped between them. "We have twelve guests who are expecting a pleasant morning without witnessing a family feud. So, how about you two kiss and make up, so to speak."

"Know what, Millie?" Amanda propped her hands on her hips.

"You love me even though I'm a thorn in your backside?"

Amanda dropped her arms to her side and burst out laughing. "I might actually miss you after you move back into your house."

"No might about it. You'll definitely miss me."

By the time they delivered first-class hospitality to Hilltop's guests then attended a church service with Erica and Millie, Amanda had abandoned the idea of a nap. Back at the ranch house, she brewed a pot of coffee while Erica and Millie prepared BLT sandwiches.

Ten minutes before Awesam's CFO was due to arrive, Millie headed to her room to feed her cats. Amanda placed her open laptop on the table then joined Erica in the kitchen. "We need to tell Wendy about the mystery reservation today during our board meeting."

"I know." Erica carried four bottles of water to the dining room table and placed them beside a plate of freshly baked cookies. "At least Millie will be in on this situation from the beginning."

"If the woman is who we suspect she is, we're in for three interesting days."

"Tension-laced is a better description than interesting."

The kitchen door swung open. Wendy waltzed in with her laptop tucked under her arm. She sniffed. "Chocolate-chip cookies. Yum." She set her laptop on the table. "How did everything go at breakfast?"

"Perfect after Amanda and I made nice with each other." Millie ambled in and set her iPad on the table.

Wendy pulled out a chair. "Will you two ever stop squabbling?"

"I doubt it." Amanda sat beside Millie and thumped her arm. "But we love each other."

"At least until one of us has a man in our life." Millie returned the arm thump. "I don't know of any other unhitched, middle-aged redheads in Blue Ridge. Which means you have a few more years to attract a guy—"

"Know what, Millie?" Amanda leaned close as if she was seconds away from revealing a secret. "I wouldn't be surprised if there's an old codger somewhere in North Georgia who would love to climb into bed with an award-winning chef who would fix him a delicious breakfast every morning."

Millie's face turned a bright shade of pink.

Amanda patted her own shoulder.

Wendy giggled. "Maybe you should both join one of those online dating sites."

"Now that we have the antics out of the way—" Erica leaned forward. "I'm calling this meeting to order. Beginning with a financial update."

"We were having so much fun. On to business." Wendy tapped her keyboard. "Since the beginning of the year, our occupancy rate has remained around seventy percent. Good news for our bottom line. Every suite is reserved for Valentine's Day weekend."

Millie tapped her iPad. "One of the couples reserved a private dinner on Valentine's Day. Bernie volunteered to help me serve."

"Speaking of Bernie—" Amanda faced Millie. "Given how hard you work, especially since we've added a private dinner option—"

"You're suggesting Bernie take over my chef duties at least one or two days a week, aren't you?"

Amanda's brows raised. *Had Bernie told her about their conversation?*

"Don't look so surprised. Bernie's a friend who doesn't keep secrets from me."

Amanda cleared her throat. "Look, we're not saying you aren't capable of working seven mornings a week—"

"Or that you aren't the most talented chef in Blue Ridge," added Erica.

"I'm only twenty-four—" Wendy tucked her long blonde hair behind her ear. "and I couldn't work every day without a break to refresh."

The three women who had changed their name from the 'exclusive wives club' to the 'victory sorority' continued to present their case until Millie raised her hand. "Do you realize you've spent the last fifteen minutes pitching Bernie without once asking me what I want? A total waste of time, because Bernie and I already agreed she'd take over every Monday and Tuesday beginning tomorrow. Also, since she also shouldn't work seven days a week, one of you ladies needs to take over her housekeeping duties every Wednesday and Thursday."

Amanda raised a brow. "You enjoyed listening to the three of us carry on, didn't you?"

A mischievous grin sent a twinkle to Millie's eyes. "I haven't had this much fun since Christmas."

Wendy reached for a cookie. "I bet there isn't an executive board on the planet that's as weird as ours."

"Now that we've established our peculiarities, I need to share something Erica and I discovered about a woman scheduled to check in Friday." Amanda tapped her keyboard then turned her laptop toward Wendy. "Her name is Donna Hewitt...from Hilton Head."

Millie's brows scrunched. "What's the big deal about her?"

Wendy stared at the screen then explained.

"Are you serious?" Millie drummed her fingers. "First Erica's ex shows up and now him?"

Amanda faced Millie. "We don't know if Donna's coming with or without her husband."

Wendy uncapped a bottle of water. "Whether she is or isn't, the reservation isn't a coincidence."

An hour after the meeting ended, Wendy strode from the garage, through the kitchen, and into the great room. Ryan was sitting on a mat playing with multi-shaped plastic blocks. Duke sprawled on the floor beside the mat.

Chris lifted off the sofa and pulled her into his arms. "How was your meeting?"

She breathed in the lingering scent of his aftershave. "More than a little strange."

He chuckled. "The same as every Awesam board meeting?"

"Not exactly." She pulled away. "First, Millie agreed to take two days a week off. Then Erica showed me an unopened ring box from Brad that no one knows about except me and Amanda. Oh, and to top everything off, Douglas Hewitt's wife reserved a Hilltop suite for the end of the week."

"Hold on." Chris gripped her shoulders. "Your father's wife?"

"Her name's Donna. We have no idea if she's coming with Douglas or by herself. One fact is certain. One or both of them intends to confront me."

"Not without me present."

Wendy tilted her head. "As my husband or my lawyer?"

"Both." Chris grabbed his ringing phone off the coffee table. "Vincent Adams. I need to take this call." He slid his finger across the screen then headed toward their office.

She lowered onto the mat beside her son, images of the day Wendy first met Vincent playing in her mind. Sitting across the table from the private investigator in the Armstrong law firm conference room where she revealed memories from the years before Cynthia abandoned her. The announcement weeks later that Vincent had located her mother.

Ryan crawled onto Wendy's lap. She wrapped her arms around her son. "I wonder if you will ever meet either of your maternal grandparents."

He babbled while reaching for a heart-shaped block.

"You're right, sweet boy. You have Nana Amanda, Grandma Linda, and Grandpa Keith to love on you. They're our real family."

Chapter 7

Erica's stomach churned as she leafed through a *People* magazine in Dr. Kennedy's waiting room. Hopefully, they'd receive encouraging news about Abby's progress. She stole a quick glance at her daughter sitting in her wheelchair tapping her phone. Did her relaxed demeanor accurately reflect her emotions, or was she putting on a show? Erica scanned the five other people in the room. What was going through their minds as they waited their turn? Erica blinked then forced her eyes to focus on a mundane article about a celebrity she had never heard of. Minutes passed.

"Abby Nelson."

The voice broke through the fog in Erica's head. She tossed the magazine aside. Her pulse accelerated as she stood and followed Abby. The jovial nurse showered her daughter with compliments while leading them down the hall and into an examination room. She settled in front of a monitor and tapped the keyboard then asked the same questions she'd asked during their last three visits. After typing Abby's responses, she scooted away from the monitor. "Dr. Kennedy will be in shortly."

While Abby refocused her attention to her phone, Erica peered at a landscape painting depicting a sunlit path winding through a lush forest. A fist-sized lump formed in her throat. Would her child ever again be able to hike in the woods or dance with Tommy?

Dr. Kennedy walked in, smiling. "How's my favorite patient?"

Abby pocketed her phone. "I've perfected the art of moving in and out of this chair."

"I wouldn't have expected anything less." He sat on a wheeled stool and moved close to her.

"I know the drill." Abby bent over and removed the sock and sneaker from her right foot.

"Impressive." Dr. Kennedy lifted her foot onto his knee. "Tell me what you feel." He ran his finger along the top of her foot.

"Same as last time, like you brushed a feather across my skin. Now for test number two." Abby's face scrunched. Her big toe moved a bit more than it had during their last visit.

"Good job." After slipping her sock and sneaker back on and returning Abby's foot to the footrest, her doctor wheeled his stool in front of the monitor and tapped the keyboard.

Erica fidgeted.

Abby twirled a lock of dark hair around her finger.

"There's been a slight improvement since your last CAT scan."

Erica blinked. "What do you mean by slight?"

"I'll show you." He turned the screen toward them revealing side-by-side images.

Erica struggled to understand as he explained in detailed medical terms the differences between the two. Would those images ever make sense?

Dr. Kennedy paused. "In other words, Abby is making progress."

"Are you saying my daughter will walk again?"

"With enough time, Abby's prospect of a full recovery is well above average."

What percentage did he consider well above average? Seventy? Eighty? Erica laced her fingers on her lap. If she asked, would his response be the same as it was during their last visit? Only one way to find out. "How much time?"

The compassion in his eyes spoke volumes. "Spinal cord healing is a slow process, which makes an accurate timetable impossible to predict."

Erica forced her expression to remain neutral. At what point would his answer change?

Dr. Kennedy scooted his stool closer to Abby. "I want you to continue therapy three times a week."

"You mean torture sessions?" She smiled. "Actually, they're kind of fun, mostly because my physical therapist has a cool sense of humor."

"Laughter is always good medicine. How are your job and college courses going?"

"Really good." Abby grinned. "Wheelchair rides are a big hit with the little kids staying at the crisis center. I think I'll name this 'Abby's Hotrod Racer.' Although I haven't figured out how to do a wheelie."

Her doctor laughed. "I wouldn't bet against you mastering that move. Other than how to perform wheelchair tricks, do you have any questions?"

"Nope."

"What about you, Ms. Nelson?"

Erica blinked, the image of her child racing down the crisis center hall on two wheels flashing across her mind. "Is a wheelchair wheelie even possible?"

"I'm counting on Abby figuring that out. I'll see you again in six weeks." He stood and pushed his stool aside. "In the meantime, keep that positive attitude, Abby."

She saluted him. "Yes, sir."

He held the door open

Abby steered her chair out to the hall and turned toward the waiting room.

Erica moved to the door.

Dr. Kennedy smiled at her. "You've raised an exceptional young woman, Ms. Nelson."

"Yes, I know." Erica stepped into the hall, then paused. Was her child's doctor a man of faith? She faced him. "I understand the importance of therapy, Dr. Kennedy, but I also believe in the power of prayer."

His eyes met hers. "So do I."

Erica choked back tears as she turned and hastened to the waiting room.

A gentleman opened the exit door for Abby.

"Thank you, sir."

"You're welcome, young lady."

Abby wheeled out to the lobby and onto the exit.

Erica followed her daughter through the automatic doors. Outside, she donned her coat and sunglasses then walked beside Abby. "What do you say we stop for lunch before I take you back to work?"

"How about Masseria?"

Erica opened the passenger door. "Let me guess. You're in the mood for pizza."

"Always."

After Abby lifted onto the passenger seat, Erica stowed her chair in the trunk then slid behind the steering wheel. Resisting the urge to discuss their appointment with Dr. Kennedy, she backed out of the parking space. "Hopefully we're ahead of the lunch crowd."

"Good, because I'm starving." Abby pulled her phone from her pocket and tapped the screen.

Erica turned onto the street, then braked at a red light. An elderly couple ambled across the intersection. Were they locals or tourists? Would Abby be able to stand and walk before summer? The light turned green. Erica forced her mind to return to the task at hand. Minutes later she pulled into a parking spot two doors down from their destination.

Abby pocketed her phone. "Tommy's gonna pick me up after work."

"All right." Erica popped the trunk then hastened behind the car. Grateful for her daughter's positive attitude, she lifted the chair to the pavement then pushed it beside the open door.

Two women walking along the sidewalk stopped and turned toward them as Abby maneuvered from the passenger seat to the chair. The taller of the two signaled a thumbs-up. "Well done, Abby."

"Thanks. Mom, meet Ms. Washburn. She was my English teacher."

Erica smiled. "It's a pleasure."

"Likewise. Your daughter was one of my smartest students." The woman's focus shifted back to Abby. "How's everything going with you and Tommy?"

"Better than ever."

"He's a bright young man with an excellent work ethic."

Erica stared at her daughter's teacher. Would she ever fully adjust to the reality of living in a small town where everyone seemed to know everyone? As soon as the women moved on by, Abby steered her chair to the entrance. Inside the cozy restaurant, the hostess led them to a table in the corner.

After ordering pizza, Abby folded her arms on the table. "We haven't talked about what's going on with you and Mr. Barkley since your last date."

Erica peered at her daughter's raised brows. Now seemed like the appropriate time to share the latest development. She leaned forward. "Something happened Saturday—"

"Oh my gosh. Did Mr. Barkley propose?"

"Not exactly." Erica relayed what happened during dinner at Brad's house.

Abby's eyes widened. "You haven't looked inside the box even one time?"

Erica shook her head.

"How can you resist peeking?"

"I promised Brad I would open the box and put the ring on my finger when I'm ready to take the next step in our relationship. Until then I don't want anything to weaken my resolve to become an independent woman who marries for no other reason than love."

Abby's head tilted. "How will you know when you're ready?"

How could she answer when she hadn't decided? Erica's mind drifted back to her childhood. "I need to tell you about a memory that surfaced during the trial." She relayed the story about Ms. Ginger.

Abby squeezed Erica's hand. "The trauma you experienced that day drove the memory deep into your subconscious to protect you. Psychology 101."

Erica nodded. "Something else I remembered. We always seemed to run out of money before the end of every month. Probably because Mother spent too much on her addiction and never stayed sober long enough to earn a living. Anyway, when the money was gone, the three of us would take the bus to the food bank and bring home enough canned goods so we wouldn't starve before the next check arrived."

Goosebumps popped out on the back of Erica's neck as a different memory began to emerge through the fog clouding her brain. "There was this one night..." She closed her eyes. "Hours after my brother and I had gone to bed in the room we shared, I heard a loud knock on our front door. I crawled out of my twin bed and opened the door a crack. Mother let a strange man come into our apartment. He followed her into her bedroom." *Number nine.* Erica gasped. Her eyes popped open. "His shirt, like some sort of sports jersey, had a big number nine on it. At first I didn't understand, and when I was older I didn't want to admit the truth. When she didn't have money, my mother traded her body for drugs. She was a weak and desperate woman."

"You're nothing like her, Mom."

"Except I married Jack to escape poverty. Then I married a con man."

"Because I wanted a daddy."

Pain erupted in the back of Erica's throat. She couldn't allow her child to shoulder even a smidgen of responsibility. "If I had been able to better provide for you, sweetheart—"

Abby placed her hand over Erica's. "I love you for trying to protect me, but I can handle the truth. Besides, if you hadn't married Gunter we wouldn't have moved to Blue Ridge, I wouldn't have met Tommy, and you wouldn't have met Mr. Barkley."

Erica marveled at her daughter's insight. "How did I manage to raise such a wise child?"

"Despite everything we've been through, you and I have always been a dynamite mother-daughter team."

Erica smiled. "Yes, we have."

"Back to the most important question of the day. When will you open that ring box?"

"When I know beyond the shadow of a doubt that the only reason to marry Brad is because I'm deeply in love with him."

Chapter 8

Pounding rain had slowed by the time Amanda waited for the last guests scheduled for Friday morning checkout to carry their luggage downstairs. Minutes later she greeted the middle-aged couple at the bottom of the front staircase. "Thank you for staying with us. We hope you enjoyed your visit."

"This was our first trip to Blue Ridge." The woman handed Amanda their room key. "Thanks to your hospitality and this lovely inn, it won't be our last."

Amanda plucked an oversized umbrella from a copper umbrella stand, then gave it to the woman's husband and opened the front door. "Leave this on the parking pad, and we'll pick it up after the rain ends."

The woman smiled. "What a thoughtful gesture."

"Our goal is to make our guests feel as if they've stayed in a friend's home."

"You've succeeded." Her husband stepped onto the porch and opened the umbrella. "This is what I call exceptional service." Shielding his wife from the drizzling rain, they descended the porch steps and hurried up the sidewalk.

Amanda pushed the door closed then stepped over to the desk. She stared at the name listed for the Bluebell Suite. Why had Wendy's stepmother reserved the only suite with twin beds? She'd find out soon enough.

"I'm ready to begin cleaning."

Amanda spun toward Bernie. "We have four rooms to prepare for new arrivals."

"I know. I checked the list when I arrived this morning."

"We're blessed to have you on our team."

"Since I began working here, I look forward to waking up every morning." Bernie's face beamed as she walked past the desk and headed up to the second story.

After taking one more glance at the check-in book, Amanda donned her jacket then grabbed her umbrella and stepped out to the porch. The drizzle mingling with cold air sent a shiver through her limbs. She scurried down the steps and headed straight to the parking pad to retrieve three umbrellas—thanks to Wendy's suggestion, another Hilltop plus. She rushed across the side yard and through the carport. Since Millie was at her house meeting with her contractor and a guest had scheduled a massage with Erica, Amanda looked forward to some time alone.

Inside the kitchen, she dropped the inn's keys into the bowl. Dusty greeted her with a tail wag. "Are you happy to see me or expecting a treat?" Abby's dog responded with a muffled bark. "I recognize that response." After tossing a treat to their canine family member, Amanda moseyed to the den and dropped onto the sofa. How long did she have before the first new guests arrived? Wendy and Chris had decided they wouldn't show up unless Donna Hewitt and whoever she was with asked to see her.

Dusty padded in and sprawled on the floor beside the coffee table.

Hoping to make the time pass quickly, Amanda grabbed the historical novel she had begun reading two days ago. By the third paragraph, she closed her eyes, her mind transported to the days when the United States began recovering from the Great Depression.

The back door opened followed by footsteps padding the kitchen floor. "What's the latest?" Millie's voice.

Amanda opened her eyes. "What do you suppose life was like toward the end of the twenty-nine depression?"

"Less depressing, I suppose." Millie plopped beside her. "You'll be happy to hear that next Tuesday my cats and I will move back home."

"Good for you." Hoping she wouldn't come across as thrilled with the news, Amanda offered a half smile. "You made it before Valentine's Day."

"In a way, I'll be moving into a brand-new house."

Erica moseyed in and dropped onto a club chair. "One massage finished, one more in an hour."

Amanda bookmarked her page. "Millie's house will be move-in ready Tuesday."

Erica grinned. "I know you're eager to return to your home."

"Finally, Whiskers and Mittens will be let out of guest-room jail." Millie crossed one leg over the other. "Do you have massages scheduled this weekend?"

"One tomorrow at four." Erica's brows raised. "Why?"

"Forty years have passed since I last shopped for furniture. Which is why I need someone with your decorating skills to help me pick out pieces to replace what I lost in the fire."

"I'll be happy to help you tomorrow morning."

"Thank you. Now, about today's new arrivals—" Millie nudged Amanda's arm. "I want to keep you company during today's check-ins."

"Who do you think you're kidding?" Amanda rolled her eyes. "What you really want is to spy on Donna Hewitt."

Millie huffed. "My responsibility as Awesam's chief information officer—at least until you actually have a computer technology system—is to identify actions that place our partners or our guests at risk."

"Give it a break, Millie. Donna Hewitt isn't some sort of criminal."

"Why do you think Donna didn't tell Wendy she'd made a reservation? Because she's the one who wants to do all the spying, that's why."

"Now you're being ridiculous." Amanda tossed her book aside and headed to the kitchen.

Millie followed her. "Maybe I'm overreacting a little—"

Amanda's brows arched. "A little?"

Erica joined them. "Actually, Millie being with you is a good idea."

Millie nodded toward Awesam's CEO. "At least Erica understands my role."

"Look," Erica faced Amanda. "We don't know who will show up with Mrs. Hewitt or the reason she made the reservation. Which makes four eyes and four ears better than two."

"All right, you can help greet our new arrivals." Amanda thumped Millie's arm. "As our silent partner."

Millie scoffed. "How can I greet anyone if I can't talk?"

"With a smile and nothing more than 'welcome to Hilltop' comments."

"All right." Millie waggled her finger at Amanda. "But I intend to keep a close eye on the situation."

"I'm sure you will." Amanda removed sandwich makings from the fridge. "For now, how about some lunch."

An hour and a half after the partners finished eating, the first guests announced their arrival. Amanda and Millie rushed to the front porch to greet the young couple from North Carolina. By four-fifteen Wendy had called three times, and everyone except the anticipated guests had checked in. After escorting the latest couple to the Butterfly Suite, Amanda joined Millie in Hilltop's kitchen.

Their chef sat on an island stool in front of her iPad. "Maybe Mrs. Hewitt changed her mind about coming."

"I checked the website this morning. She hasn't canceled." Amanda sat beside her. "Have you decided what style of furniture you want to buy?"

"Clever move, changing the subject."

"Did it work?"

"Nope." The front doorbell rang. "That's them." Millie slid off her stool.

Amanda grabbed her arm. "Remember—"

"Stop worrying." Millie yanked her arm from Amanda's grip. "I won't embarrass you."

Amanda hesitated, then headed to the foyer with Millie following close behind. She opened the door and faced an attractive, elegantly dressed woman. "Welcome to Hilltop Inn. I'm Amanda, one of the inn's owners. I assume you're Ms. Hewitt."

"Your assumption is correct." The woman pulled her designer suitcase into the foyer.

Amanda peered around her. "Is someone joining you?"

"I'm here alone."

Millie inched forward and eyed the woman from head to toe. "I'm Mildred Cunningham, Hilltop's award-winning chef. Are you visiting Blue Ridge to rest or to shop?"

Mrs. Hewitt eyed Millie with more than a hint of irritation. "Neither."

"We're delighted you've chosen to stay with us. Please come sign our guest book." Amanda shot Millie her sternest warning expression while their guest signed the book. When she finished, Millie tagged close behind Amanda while she showed their new guest around the common areas and shared details about the inn. Reluctant to ask if she had questions, Amanda led the way back to the foyer. "I'll meet you upstairs in a moment." She waited until their guest reached the top step then pulled Millie aside. "You stay down here—"

"But—"

"This isn't up for discussion."

"Hmph."

Amanda grabbed the room key then headed up to the second-story hall extending the full length of the inn. "You've reserved a lovely room." She unlocked the Bluebell Suite and handed over the key. "Please let us know if there is anything we can do to make your stay exceptional."

"I will." She pulled her luggage into the room.

Amanda gripped the door handle.

"There is one thing." Donna Hewitt spun toward her. "Wendy Thomason is one of the inn's owners, correct?"

"Yes. She's our chief financial officer, except her name is Wendy Armstrong now."

"I'd like you to arrange a meeting between the two of us."

Amanda's eyes remained trained on Mrs. Hewitt's impassive expression. "May I tell her why?"

The woman hesitated. "Tell her I'm here to meet my husband's daughter."

There it was. The real reason for her visit. "I'll contact Wendy."

"Thank you." Their guest turned away and pulled her suitcase to a luggage stand.

Amanda pulled the door closed then returned to the stairs.

Millie waited for her at the bottom step, her arms crossed. "Well?"

Amanda descended. "She wants to meet with Wendy."

"I'm telling you, that woman is up to no good."

"Don't go jumping to conclusions, Millie." Amanda grabbed her phone off the desk and pressed Wendy's number.

The spicy aroma of homemade chili wafted through the great room as Wendy glanced at her phone for the umpteenth time. Five minutes had passed since she'd last checked. Why hadn't Donna Hewitt checked in? Was she running late? Had she changed her mind? Wendy checked the Hilltop website. No cancellations. After setting her laptop on the coffee table, Wendy pocketed her phone then turned up the music to help drown out the noise in her head. She lifted Ryan off the floor. "Your daddy will be home soon."

"Dada?"

"Who loves you so much." Wendy smiled, grateful their son's first word had honored Chris. She lowered their little guy into the playpen beside the kitchen counter then removed romaine lettuce and a bottle of Caesar dressing from the fridge.

Wendy startled at Amanda's ringtone. Her heart pounding, she yanked her phone from her pocket and swiped her finger across the screen. "Has she checked in? Who's with her?"

"Ten minutes ago, and she's alone."

If she'd planned to come alone, why did she reserve the room with twin beds? "What's she like? Does she know who I am?"

"She's what you'd expect—a woman of means, and yes, she knows you're her husband's daughter." Amanda paused. "She wants to meet with you in private."

Wendy's pulse accelerated as she leaned back against the counter. "Did she say why?"

"Not really."

A litany of potential reasons raced through Wendy's mind at warp speed. Did her father know what was going on? Did he approve?

"What do you want me to do?"

Wendy blinked. "Tell her I'll meet her in the inn's dining room tomorrow at noon." She ended the call. Chances were Douglas Hewitt had no idea his wife was hours away from secretly meeting his daughter. Now all she had to do was convince Chris to let her talk to Donna alone.

Chapter 9

Twenty minutes before the scheduled meeting, Wendy peered at Hilltop's front porch as Chris drove up the ranch house driveway and parked behind Abby's car. "Thank you for trusting me to meet with Donna Hewitt alone."

"You've already overcome more challenges than a lot of people endure in their entire lives. You're more than capable of dealing with your father's wife." Chris reached across the console and squeezed her hand. "However, if any legal issues surface, your attorney will be thirty seconds away."

Wendy patted his cheek. "I was smart to marry a brilliant lawyer."

He winked. "Yeah, you were." Chris motioned toward Millie standing in the kitchen threshold vigorously motioning to them. "If we don't go in, she's likely to go bonkers."

Wendy giggled. "Is that some sort of newfangled legal term?"

"Only as it applies to Hilltop's overzealous chef." He climbed out, then lifted his sleeping son from his car seat and cradled him in his arms.

Wendy stepped onto the pavement and buttoned her royal blue suit jacket then headed to the door where Millie stood.

"I made sure the inn's dining room is all set for your private meeting." Millie moved aside.

"Hmm." Wendy crossed the threshold. "Did you also install hidden cameras?"

Millie sneered. "Bernie and I don't need a camera to keep an eye on our guests."

Chris carried Ryan inside. "Somehow spying doesn't seem to fit Hilltop's definition of hospitality."

"You're a smart lawyer, so you should know observing is a long way from spying." Millie spun away then strode to the den.

Wendy and Chris followed and joined Erica at the dining room table. Millie settled on the chair across from Wendy and drummed her fingers. "Do you want to know what we observed during breakfast?"

Wendy shrugged. "You might as well tell us."

Millie crossed her arms on the table. "First off, Donna didn't show up until after half the guests had finished eating. Even though other guests tried to talk to her, she barely uttered two words. She only ate half her breakfast but drank two cups of coffee."

"Well, now." Wendy rolled her eyes. "There's a bit of earth-shattering news."

"I'm just saying the woman who's married to your father acted as jittery as an old dog confronted by a ticked-off kitty."

Chris cocked a brow. "Do you suppose two women watching her like hawks searching for prey might have influenced her demeanor?"

Millie huffed. "Ask Amanda when you see her. She knows Bernie and I weren't obvious."

"Now that you've given Wendy an update—" Erica scooted her chair away from the table. "We need to leave if we're going to do any serious shopping before my four o'clock massage appointment."

"All right." Millie waggled her finger at Wendy. "As Awesam's chief information officer, I'll expect a full account of your meeting as soon as we return." She grabbed her purse off the back of her chair and followed Erica through the kitchen then out the back door.

Amanda meandered in from the hall. "How has my grandson managed to sleep through all this commotion?"

"A ten-minute car ride is the perfect tranquilizer."

"Hopefully, he'll wake up soon." Amanda sat beside Chris. "In case you're wondering, Millie has perfected the art of subtle observation."

Wendy's brows peaked. "Oh my gosh, are you actually defending her?"

"Only when logic dictates." Amanda settled beside Wendy. "You're the perfect picture of a successful executive."

Chris nodded. "Successful and confident."

"Thanks to my attorney prepping me for all possible scenarios." Wendy tucked her hair behind her ear revealing diamond studs. "At least no one can accuse me and my Victory Sorority Sisters of leading dull lives."

Chris chuckled. "Maybe someone should write a book about you three."

"Talk about a dramedy."

Ryan raised his head off his daddy's chest. "I think our little guy is ready to snuggle with his nana." Chris placed his son in Amanda's arms.

"Hey, sweet boy." Amanda carried him to the blanket she had laid on the floor beside the fireplace.

Wendy raised a brow as she lifted Hilltop's pinging phone off the table. "A text from Donna Hewitt. She wants to know if I'm on my way. It's ten minutes before our scheduled meeting time."

Amanda peered over her shoulder. "Donna is either eager or anxious."

"Probably a little of both," added Chris.

Wendy texted a response. "I told her I'm on my way."

"I'll walk you to the door." Chris wrapped his arm around her shoulders as they made their way to the kitchen. "Time to turn on your Wendy charm."

Wendy grabbed the inn's key off the counter. "Thank you for being my cheerleader, darling."

"Always." Chris kissed her cheek.

Wendy hummed a tune to ease her anxiety and headed across the side yard then up the inn's front sidewalk. She stopped humming, climbed onto the front porch, and unlocked the door. Gripping the handle, she breathed deeply then stepped into the foyer and peered into the living room. An attractive woman wearing a casual outfit stood in front of the book stand leafing through the inn's scrapbook. "Mrs. Hewitt?"

She stepped away from the book stand. "I assume you're Wendy Armstrong."

"I am." The aroma of freshly baked cookies wafted across the space as Wendy escorted her to the dining room. She closed the pocket doors and motioned toward a chair. "Please have a seat."

"Thank you."

Wendy sat catercorner to her stepmother. Now what? Wait for her to start the conversation or jump right in?

Donna Hewitt peered around the room.

Time to take charge. "I hope you're enjoying your stay."

"Hilltop is a first-class inn with an interesting story."

"Transforming this house from a private residence has been a labor of love for me and my partners."

"Well worth the effort." Donna twisted the cap off a bottle of water and took a sip. "How much do you know about Douglas Hewitt?"

Wendy blinked. The woman got right to the point.

"There's no point pretending you don't know who I'm talking about."

Relax and trust your instincts. "Only that during a spring break in Biloxi, Mississippi, he had a one-night stand with my mother, and now he's involved in real estate."

"The family business is one of the most successful real-estate investment firms in the Southeast."

No false humility there. "How did you find out about me?"

Donna fingered her wedding ring. "Last summer I overheard our housekeeper on her phone telling someone that you and your attorney had shown up at our home while our sons and I were out of town. When I confronted her, she told me she had heard your entire conversation with my husband." Donna pulled a business card from her pocket and laid it on the table. "After you left, she retrieved this from the trash."

Wendy lifted the card and stared at her name, Wendy Thomason. "My attorney proposed to me that same day." She held up her left hand. "Now he's my husband."

"Congratulations."

Wendy dropped the card on the table. "I hope your housekeeper didn't lose her job."

"For telling me the truth?"

"Only after you overheard her."

"She's been part of our family since our boys were born. Besides, you showing up at our home wasn't her fault." Donna paused. "Have you contacted Douglas since your first visit?"

"He made it clear he had no interest in a relationship with me, so I haven't bothered. Does he know about your conversation with your housekeeper?"

No response.

"I'm not trying to pry into your personal life."

Donna sighed as her eyes met Wendy's. "Douglas and I haven't been close for years."

"Are you saying he doesn't know?"

"You're a bright young woman. You figure it out. Did your mother tell you she'd had an affair with Douglas?"

Wendy's lips tightened. "The truth is my mother had no idea who my father was. Until last spring, I hadn't had any contact with her since I was five years old."

Donna lifted a brow. "Who raised you?"

"A series of foster parents."

"I'm sorry."

Wendy shrugged. "You don't need to feel sorry for me. Now my life is more wonderful than I ever imagined it could be."

Her father's wife stared at her for a long moment. "How old are you?"

"Twenty-four."

Donna broke eye contact. "Which means you were conceived while Douglas was in college."

"I assume you knew him back then."

Tight lines framed the woman's mouth. "Your assumption is correct." Donna reached for a cookie. "Your staff obviously knows who I am."

So much for Millie's subtle snooping. Wendy crossed one leg over the other. "You've known about me for months. Why did you wait so long to meet me?"

Donna swallowed a bite of cookie. "Three years after my second son was born, I miscarried. Losing the daughter I always wanted broke my heart. I was never able to conceive again." Her eyes reddened. "I'm here because even though you're not my flesh and blood, you're my sons' half-sister and my stepdaughter."

What? Wendy hadn't expected such a vulnerable response. She reached across the corner of the table and touched Donna's arm. "I hope my second child is a girl."

"Your second?" Donna's brows raised. "Are you saying I have a grandchild?"

Wendy tilted her head. "Didn't your housekeeper tell you I was pregnant when I came to your house?"

"She obviously failed to reveal that little detail."

"Your grandson's name's Ryan. Would you like to meet him?"

"You don't mind?"

"A boy can't have too many grandmothers." Wendy stood. "He's next door with his daddy."

"One fact is clear." Donna Hewitt lifted off her chair. "My husband's refusal to acknowledge you is his loss."

"Maybe one day he'll change his mind." Wendy led the way to the foyer and out the front door. "Do you plan to tell him we've met?"

"If and when I decide he deserves to know."

They made their way to the carport and into the ranch house den. "Darling, and Nana Amanda, meet our little guy's Hilton Head grandmother."

Chris exchanged a quick glance with Amanda, then lifted off a club chair and extended his hand. "Chris Armstrong. It's a pleasure."

She accepted. "Donna Hewitt. Likewise."

With Ryan in her arms, Amanda rose from the other club chair. "Would you like to hold your grandson?"

"Will he mind a stranger holding him?"

"You won't be a stranger for long."

While Amanda placed Ryan in Donna's arms, Chris excused himself and led Wendy through the kitchen and out to the carport. "Your charm obviously worked some magic."

"I don't know if she's here because she wants me to replace the daughter she lost or to defy my father." Wendy relayed their conversation.

"Whatever her motivation, the only thing that matters is what happens beginning today."

"You're right. Should we invite her to dinner to let you put your attorney skills to work?"

Chris grinned. "I'll leave that decision in your hands."

"In that case..." Wendy led the way back inside. Donna and Amanda sat on the sofa with Ryan sitting between them playing with a toy. "I'd like to invite you to join Chris and me for dinner tonight."

"I appreciate the offer." Donna peered up at Wendy. "However, my college roommate is driving over from Chattanooga to spend the next couple of days with me."

That explained why she had reserved the suite with twin beds. "Before you leave Blue Ridge, you're invited to come by our house for another visit with your grandson."

"Thank you." A smile lit Donna's face. "I accept."

Ninety minutes after Donna left and Wendy and Chris drove home, Millie dashed through the kitchen, plopped onto a club chair across from Amanda, and set her phone on the end table. "What's the scoop on Donna Hewitt? Does her husband know she's here?"

Amanda's brow pinched. "Where's Erica?"

"With a massage customer." Millie crossed one leg over the other. "How did Donna find out about Wendy, and why did she want to meet her?"

Time for some fun. "How'd your furniture shopping trip go? Did you find everything you were looking for?"

Millie's eyes narrowed. "You're toying with me, aren't you?"

"A little."

"If you won't tell me—" Hilltop's chef yanked her phone off the end table. "I'll call Wendy."

"Relax already. I'm just having a little fun at your expense."

"Well?" Millie pumped her foot. "Are you or aren't you going to tell me what happened?"

"First, Ryan now has one more grandmother to love on him. And second, even though her husband doesn't know she's here, Donna intends to have a relationship with Wendy. Which means tomorrow you won't need to spy on her, understood? By the way, she knew you were watching her this morning."

Millie huffed. "Because I wanted her to know."

"Sure you did." Amanda's tone mocked.

"All right. I admit I need to work on being a little more subtle."

"A little more subtle?"

Millie huffed. "A lot more." She paused. "You know you ladies are my family, which is why I'll do whatever is needed to protect you and our business."

"Know what, Millie? We're glad you're Awesam's pistol-packing mama bear."

Millie grinned. "Yeah, I know."

Chapter 10

The scent of freshly brewed coffee wafted through the space while Wendy rinsed the breakfast plates and placed them in the dishwasher. "In thirty minutes, Donna Hewitt will drive through our wooded lot and park in front of our house—a stark contrast to her grand manor and its manicured front lawn."

"Blue Ridge rustic versus Hilton Head formal." Chris set his mug on the granite countertop serving as a breakfast bar in their kitchen anchoring one end of their great room.

"The first time I drove up your driveway, I expected the inside to look like the outside. Then you opened the front door." Wendy swept her arm toward the smooth cream-colored walls and vaulted ceiling. "Imagine how surprised I was at how different the upscale inside was from the log cabin facade."

"Just like some people."

"Know what?" Wendy skirted the counter and straightened Chris's tie. "That's the same comment you made that day."

"Seems I need new material."

Ryan crawled over from his playmat. Chris slid off his stool and lifted their little guy into his arms. He blew a raspberry on his son's neck, triggering a bout of belly laughs. "Daddy has to go brush his teeth before he heads to court to defend a client."

Ryan touched his face. "Dada."

A smile sent a twinkle to Chris's eyes. "You're the smartest little guy on the planet."

Wendy's heart overflowed with joy as her child's daddy placed their son in her arms. "Your daddy is the smartest and sweetest guy in the world." While Chris headed to their bedroom, Wendy carried Ryan to his playmat between the coffee table and fireplace. She lit a candle on the mantel, releasing a beachy sandalwood scent, then stepped back and peered at the large flatscreen television over the fireplace.

Chris slipped up beside Wendy and slid his arm around her waist. "What's going through your brilliant brain?"

"I didn't know beans about football when we met. Thanks to your enthusiasm for the game—"

"And my expert instruction."

She brushed her fingers through his hair. "Now, I'm almost as big a fan as your family."

"God, family, and football—the perfect combination for a proper southern clan."

Wendy smiled. "When's the last time I told you how much I love you?"

"Last night." He winked. "As much as I'd love to stay and show you how much I love you, I have to go earn a living." He kissed Wendy's cheek then grabbed his briefcase and headed toward the garage.

As soon as the back door closed, Wendy turned on background music. After she finished cleaning up the kitchen, she took one last glance around. Satisfied everything was in place, she settled on the sofa. Ryan crawled over, gripped her pant leg, and pulled up. "It won't be long before you take your first step." Their little guy babbled then plopped onto his diaper-clad fanny. Wendy grinned. "I'm glad you agree."

Duke's ears perked followed by a muffled bark.

"Seems your Hilton Head grandma has arrived." Wendy lifted Ryan off the floor, then followed their black Lab. Her pulse accelerated the moment she pulled the front door open.

Donna, wearing designer jeans, three-inch heels, and a gold pullover sweater, slid out of a late model BMW. "What a lovely setting, so private and peaceful."

"This is typical for the North Georgia mountains, although they're more like rolling hills." Was her father's wife one of those people who was different on the inside than she was on the outside? "Love your outfit."

"I bought everything except the shoes yesterday." Donna stepped onto the porch then walked inside. "This isn't at all what I expected from the exterior."

"Everyone's surprised the first time they walk in."

Ryan giggled.

"Our little guy's happy to see you." Duke's wagging tail made it clear he approved of their guest. "So is our four-legged family member. His name's Duke."

"Hello, Duke." Donna patted the dog's head then held up a gift bag. "I brought Ryan a couple of presents. Both are educational."

"How sweet." Wendy pushed the door closed. "Would you like a cup of coffee?"

"No thank you. I filled up during breakfast."

Wendy led her guest through the great room and motioned toward the brown leather sofa facing the fireplace.

After settling on one end, Donna placed the gift bag on the coffee table. "It seems like only a short time ago my boys were Ryan's age, and now they're both teenagers."

"Everyone says they grow up fast." Wendy lowered her child onto his playmat while Duke sprawled on the floor between the mat and fireplace.

"Thank you for the gifts." She removed a touch-and-feel book and an interactive plush bear from the bag.

"I hope he doesn't already have either."

"He doesn't. Ryan will love both." She placed the gifts on the mat. Duke sniffed the toys before nudging the bear toward Ryan with his muzzle.

"The bear obviously meets with your dog's approval."

"Duke has taken on the role of our little guy's friend and protector." Wendy sat on the other end of the sofa. "I hope you and your college roommate enjoyed your stay in Blue Ridge."

"Both of us were impressed with Hilltop Inn as well as the charming stores."

"Most days there are more tourists than locals downtown. Before I met Chris, I lived in a condo on the beach in Gulfport, Mississippi."

"Do you miss living on the coast?"

"When I first moved to Blue Ridge, I missed the sound of the surf and the smell of salty sea air. Now I wouldn't want to live anywhere else."

"Because you're happy here." Donna lifted a photo of Wendy, Chris, and Ryan off the end table. "You have a beautiful family."

Wendy smiled. "Thank you."

"I'm curious." Donna set the photo back on the table. "You were pregnant when you showed up at my home last spring."

"Yes." So she'd done the math. "Which is one reason Chris drove me to Hilton Head."

"Because you wanted your attorney present?"

Wendy nodded. "We didn't know how Douglas would react to discovering he had a daughter."

"Smart move." Donna faced Wendy, her brows raised. "Why did the father of your child wait so long to propose to you?"

Wendy's pulse accelerated. How should she respond to the woman who was still a stranger? With a version of the truth. "My ex is my son's biological father."

Donna stared wide-eyed at her. "That's why Chris accompanied you to Hilton Head as your lawyer and not your husband."

Wendy nodded. "After we married a few weeks later, Chris adopted Ryan." Her little guy crawled around the coffee table and pulled up to his feet. Wendy lifted him onto her lap. "Which makes Chris his legal father and more importantly, his daddy."

"Your husband is a good man."

"He's the best." Wendy moved Ryan to the cushion between her and Donna.

"What I told you about knowing Douglas when he had that one-night stand with your mother was only part of the truth." Donna paused for a long moment. "We had been engaged for six months when he and his buddies went on that spring-break trip."

Wendy gasped. "Oh my gosh, I'm sorry."

"I'm not telling you because I want or need your sympathy." Donna crossed her legs and pumped her foot. "You need to know because fathering you isn't the only indiscretion my husband has committed during the past twenty-five years. Douglas is a proud man who refuses to admit that he's a slave to his desires, which is why he reacted the way he did that day you showed up at our door." Donna faced Wendy. "Whether he realizes it or not, he rejected you because you're a physical reminder of his weakness."

Wendy's heart ached for her stepmother. "Knowing he's been unfaithful...why have you stayed with him?"

"I first learned he was involved with another woman when I was eight months pregnant with our second child. Afterwards I recognized all the signs." Donna's foot stilled. "The main reason I haven't left him is because he's a good father to our sons, and they adore him. Plus, exposing them to a messy divorce would break their hearts."

"You're a good mother."

"I've learned to live with my husband's infidelities and take full advantage of the lifestyle his family's wealth provides. Other than engaging in what he believes are secret affairs, Douglas has never mistreated me. Which also makes rationalizing my decision to stay in a broken marriage easier to accept."

Wendy caught her bottom lip between her teeth. This woman who had been a stranger three days earlier trusted her with painful truths. Maybe she should do the same. "What I told you about my ex being Ryan's biological father is only half of the truth."

"Was he also an unfaithful husband?"

"Unfaithful doesn't begin to describe Gunter Benson's deception." Her stepmother's mouth fell open as Wendy's details spilled out about meeting Amanda and Erica at the Blue Ridge Inn then learning they were all illegally married to the same con man. "We were forced to sell all our jewelry and most of our possessions to pay the back taxes on the two properties he had inherited."

"Where is Gunter now?"

"Serving twenty-five to life in Nevada for murder."

"Oh my stars." Donna uncrossed her legs. "Compared to Gunter, Douglas isn't such a bad husband."

"Do you plan to stay with him after your boys are grown?"

"Every anniversary I pray he'll have a change of heart and honor our marriage vows."

Wendy shrugged. "I suppose at some point we have to face the fact that most people don't change."

Donna pulled her arm off the back of the sofa. "Unless something unexpected happens."

"Such as discovering he has a grandson?" Wendy smiled as Ryan crawled onto Donna's lap and fingered her necklace. "Have you decided whether or not my father deserves to know about our visit?"

"For the past few months, I've only considered the impact on Douglas. But now, you and Ryan are part of my family."

"Are you saying you are planning to tell Douglas and your sons about this weekend?"

"I haven't decided, but I promise to let you know when I decide one way or the other. In the meantime, would you mind sending me pictures of my grandson and maybe news about little milestones?"

"You're one of our son's grandmothers. Of course I'll keep you updated."

"You're a good stepdaughter, Wendy."

She stared at Donna. How after meeting for the first time two days ago, could the woman who didn't know she'd existed six months earlier care more about her than the woman who had brought her into this world? An involuntary giggle escaped.

Donna's eyes widened.

"Sorry..." Wendy stifled the giggle. "It's just...growing up I was an only child who longed for a normal family. Now, I have two secret half-sisters, three secret half-brothers, and a secret stepmother."

Donna laughed. "We are one bizarre family."

Wendy nodded. "That, we are."

Chapter 11

Following the hour-long massage, Erica stepped into her office to allow her client a few minutes of privacy. She peered out the window above her desk, offering a view of the woods. Three deer meandered on the other side of the fence Millie had installed to prevent the animals from treating the inn's English country garden as their meal ticket. Funny how the neighbor who had threatened to stop Awesam from rezoning the property for commercial use had become one of their closest allies.

A knock interrupted the silence.

Erica opened the door and smiled at the woman visiting from Illinois. "How are you feeling?"

"Thanks to your magic hands, I'm relaxed and ready to explore Blue Ridge." She handed Erica a generous tip.

"Thank you." Erica escorted their guest out to the waiting room. "I hope you enjoy your last day with us, and please let us know if there's anything we can do for you."

"Thus far, our stay has been perfect."

"Excellent." Erica waited for the guest to leave the spa, then returned to her office and settled on her desk chair. She tapped her laptop keyboard and opened the Excel spreadsheet titled, 'goals.' Her shoulders slumped as she stared at the page which, except for a column heading, had remained blank for two days. *Why had this become such a difficult task?*

Fourteen months ago she had checked into the Blue Ridge Inn expecting to celebrate her thirty-sixth birthday with her husband. Instead she'd become acquainted with Amanda and Wendy during a blizzard then faced devastating news about the man they each believed was their husband. The con man had left each of them with foreclosed homes and mountains of unpaid bills. Unlike her mother, who coped with difficulty by ravaging her body with illicit drugs, Erica returned to Asheville and took a second part-time job as a waitress. She lifted a photo of her and Abby off the desk. If they hadn't moved to Blue Ridge, her child wouldn't be confined to a wheelchair. Her focus drifted to the Massage Institute of Cleveland diploma hanging on the wall beside the window. They'd also be struggling to survive on her meager earnings.

Erica placed the photo on the desk then ambled into the massage room and breathed in the scented candle aroma. She had told Abby she would know that Brad was her soulmate when her heart and her mind came into agreement. Brad was nothing like Jack, Gunter, or the man wearing the number nine jersey. What else did she need to accomplish before her mind could align with her heart?

The door swung open. Millie dashed in. "My new furniture is scheduled to arrive in an hour. I need you to help me arrange everything."

"I'll meet you next door in a few minutes."

"Thanks." Millie rushed out.

Erica blew out the candle flame then returned to her office. She released a heavy sigh, tapped her keyboard, and stared at the screen. Why was this taking so long? She heaved a heavy sigh, then closed the file. Deciding what she needed to accomplish would have to wait.

Amanda scooted her chair close to the dining room table and opened the Hilltop website. Tomorrow, twelve ladies from South Carolina would check into Hilltop and spend three days playing bridge. Their first big group.

Millie rushed in through the back door. "My wagon's in the carport."

"If you'd driven your car over, we wouldn't have to deal with the steep driveways."

Millie scoffed. "After the fire, I rolled my suitcase all the way over here. Believe me, I'm perfectly capable of rolling it back."

"Except you'll need to carry your cats." Amanda paused. "Actually it doesn't matter who carries or pulls what. You've waited months to move back into your home."

"You're gonna miss having me around, aren't you?"

"Yeah." Amanda grinned. "Like an itch I've grown accustomed to."

"Living here for the past few months has brought me to one undeniable conclusion—"

"That dogs are more lovable than cats?"

"Just one canine critter." Millie propped her right hand on her hip. "If I had a daughter, she'd be exactly like you."

Amanda raised a brow. "Are you boasting or complaining?"

"What do you think?"

"Mostly boasting."

Erica walked in and set her laptop on the table. "Who's bragging about what?"

"Seems I've become the daughter Millie never had."

"Hmm." Erica tapped her finger to her chin. "You two do have a few personality traits in common."

Amanda laughed. "As declared by our partner in charge of team building."

"Speaking of team." Millie lowered her hand to her side. "Are you two ready to help me move out of your guest room?"

Erica nodded. "Ready and able."

Amanda followed her partners to the room Millie had occupied for months. Mittens peeked out from under the bed while Whiskers leapt off the windowsill. "Your feline companions won't know how to act after spending all this time confined within these four walls."

Millie lifted Whiskers off the floor and placed him in the pet carrier. She pulled Mittens out from under the bed then set her beside Whiskers and zipped the carrier closed. "Vacation is over. It's time to go home." Taking the roll of drill sergeant, Millie barked instructions to Amanda and Erica, then carried her pets out to the carport.

Amanda followed and placed the litter box and a carton containing Eleanor Harrington's journals and miscellaneous items onto the wooden wagon then followed Millie down the driveway. "At least we're not dealing with rain or rivers of water and foam flowing down the road."

Erica rolled the suitcase between the truck and Abby's car. "We're lucky that lightning didn't strike the inn."

Millie glanced over her shoulder. "Or your house." They strode past Hilltop Inn, up Millie's driveway, and onto the front porch. Millie gripped the doorknob. "I remember that day Erica and Wendy first showed up on my porch. I knew the minute I opened the door and saw the plate of store-bought cookies, they were on a mission to convince me to drop the petition to stop your rezoning efforts."

"I'm curious." Amanda lifted the box off the wagon. "Would homemade cookies have won you over that afternoon?"

"Not a chance. The only thing that changed my mind was you going along with Wendy's idea to offer me the chef job." Millie opened the front door and stepped into the foyer.

Erica pulled the suitcase across the threshold. Amanda carried the box inside. Fresh air replaced every trace of smoke and charred wood. Other than a coffee table and a large box beside the new built-in bookcase anchoring the wall opposite the foyer, the living room remained empty.

Millie placed her cat carrier on the new hardwood floor then unzipped the flap and lifted Mittens into her arms. Whiskers slithered from the carrier and stretched, then headed straight to his perch on the front windowsill. "My cat is a creature of habit." Millie touched the ornate coffee table's glass inlay. "This is the only salvageable piece of furniture in this room. Too bad it's a totally different style from my new furniture."

"From a decorating perspective—" Erica ambled into the room. "Eclectic décor shows your personality."

Amanda chuckled. "You mean eccentric?"

"More like creative." Erica moved to the fireplace. "I can't believe the crew removed every bit of soot from these bricks."

"One more reason the work took so long." Millie placed Mittens on the floor then opened the large box. She removed the accessories she had cleaned a week after the fire and arranged them on the bookcase. "Will one of you bring me Eleanor's journals?"

"Sure." Amanda removed the journals from the box she'd carried over and handed them to Millie. "Some of your most prized possessions."

Tears pooled and spilled down Millie's cheeks as she placed the journals on a shelf. "I've always been a little off-putting, which is why I never had close friends until I met Eleanor." She lifted a decorative plate off the display stand and ran her finger over the verse about friendship. "She gave me this gift the last summer she spent in Blue Ridge. When she passed, I felt lost and alone. Then you two and Wendy invited me into your lives." Millie set the plate back on the stand. "Now with Bernie and your extended families, I can count more than a dozen people as friends."

Amanda slid her arm around their chef's thin shoulders. "We're more than friends; we're family."

Millie dabbed the tears tracking down her cheeks. "Sorry for the waterworks."

"No need to apologize." Erica eased beside Millie. "Moving back into your home is an emotional experience. Besides, happy tears are good tears."

A truck backing up beeped in the driveway.

Amanda lowered her arm. "Your new furniture has arrived."

Millie squared her shoulders then hurried across the room and out the front door.

Erica nudged Amanda. "Our partner transitioned from sentimental pal to demanding drill sergeant."

"This will be fun to watch." Amanda stood at the door as two men climbed from the cab.

Millie stood guard while they rolled up the rear door and lifted a sofa off the truck. "That goes inside."

The younger man shrugged. "We figured that much."

Ignoring his comment, Millie led the way into the living room. For the better part of an hour, she directed and redirected the precise placement of each piece of furniture she had purchased for the living room, kitchen, and guest room. After the men placed the last piece, she pulled two bills from her pocket and handed one to each. "Thank you for your patience."

"You're welcome, ma'am." After tipping his cap to Millie and thanking her, the older of the two men followed the younger guy out the front door.

Amanda straightened a shade on a new lamp. "Your new style is perfect."

"From formal and stuffy to casual and comfortable." Millie ran her hand along the top of her sofa. "You know what I should do now that I'm an award-winning chef with a fat bank account?"

Amanda raised a brow. "Prepare a delicious dinner to thank us for helping you move back home?"

She rolled her eyes. "Take Erica on another shopping trip to help me redecorate the master bedroom. That's for another day. About dinner tonight. Meet me here at five and bring a bottle of wine."

"Red or white?"

"Red." Millie gripped her suitcase handle then spun toward the hall. "I'll see you tonight." She flicked her hand over her shoulder as she headed toward her bedroom.

Amanda chuckled. "Sergeant Millie has dismissed the troops."

"So it seems." Erica followed Amanda out the front door and onto the sidewalk. "Do you suppose Millie devised her stop-the-rezoning petition so she could meet us?"

Amanda stared at her. "Have you forgotten what Chris first told us about her?"

Erica shrugged. "That she had too much time on her hands and a giant chip on her shoulder?"

"There's your explanation, Sherlock. Millie ending up as our partner and friend was an unexpected bonus." Amanda pulled her phone from her pocket. "Huh."

"What?"

"Keith wants me to meet him at his office tomorrow morning."

"Chris's dad?"

"None other."

"Does he say why?"

Amanda shook her head. "Since the Armstrong law firm represents our company, the meeting is most likely related to business."

"Unless Gunter has reared his ugly head again."

"If he has, wouldn't Chris be contacting us?"

"Not if he's tied up defending another client."

Chapter 12

After swallowing her last bite of beef, Erica set her fork on Millie's new kitchen table and patted her belly. "As Abby would say, dinner was scrumlicious."

Millie's face beamed. "My newest gourmet creation. What's your opinion about adding the meal to our private dining menu?"

"I think that's a great idea."

Amanda wiped her mouth with a napkin. "Have you discussed the financials with Wendy?"

"I will tomorrow." Millie moved the dinner dishes to the sink then refilled their wine glasses and lifted a plate of truffles off the counter.

Amanda wrapped her fingers around her wine glass stem. "Dark chocolate and red wine. Nice touch, Chef Millie."

"We'll enjoy dessert in my new living room." After Millie led the way from the kitchen and placed the plate on the coffee table, she ignited a gas fire in her refurbished fireplace. "The construction crew transitioned this from wood to gas."

Amanda sat on the sofa beside Erica and set her glass of wine beside the truffles. "Because gas is safer than burning wood?"

Millie nodded. "I'm not taking any chances." She settled on her new recliner and set her wine glass on the table beside her chair.

Erica plucked a truffle off the platter. "Gunter's gift to Wendy."

Millie's brow pinched. "What are you talking about?"

"When the three of us first checked into the Blue Ridge Inn, Gunter had ordered a bottle of Champagne for Amanda, chardonnay for me, and a box of truffles for Wendy. After we discovered we were all married to the con man, we commiserated by consuming his gifts in the inn's library." Erica bit into the truffle. "This is delicious."

Millie stared at Erica. "The time has come for you to fess up, Ms. Nelson."

Erica swallowed. "Confess what?"

"You haven't uttered a single word about Brad Barkley the entire day. What's going on? Are you still together, or did you break up? Are you still fretting over Abby's accident?"

Erica's back stiffened. "Nothing has changed between Brad and me. We're simply letting our relationship evolve naturally."

Millie's brows raised. "As opposed to unnaturally?"

Amanda crossed her arms. "Give Erica a break, Millie. She and Brad don't want to rush into anything."

Millie's eyes shifted from Amanda back to Erica. "Does Awesam's president know something I don't?"

Erica swallowed the last bite of truffle. She didn't dare tell Millie about the ring hidden in her dresser drawer, but their inquisitive chef would never believe some made-up explanation. She had no choice other than telling a version of the truth. "Brad's heart shattered when cancer stole his wife from him."

"A lot of time has passed since Jan died."

"Time doesn't heal all wounds, Millie. Besides, I'm still recovering from one abusive and one illegal marriage. Which is why we're taking one day at a time."

"I suppose in your mind dragging your feet makes sense." Millie waggled her finger at Erica. "Given Brad's handsome looks and eligibility, I wouldn't dillydally around too long."

"Point taken." Erica took a sip of wine. "Now it's my turn to be inquisitive."

Millie raised her chair's footrest. "About my nonexistent love life?"

"That would be an interesting topic; however, I'm curious about what you called your fat bank account."

Millie stared at Erica for a long moment. "You really are nosey."

Amanda uncrossed her arms then reached for her wine. "So am I. So, what gives?"

"You remember I told you that Rupert and I both worked retail, right?"

"Yes," Erica and Amanda answered in unison.

"Despite the fact that neither of us ever held high-paying jobs, we paid all our bills on time and furnished every room in our little house with garage and estate-sale bargains. We even managed to put money away every month for our son's college education. Sadly, Rupert passed on shortly after we paid off our mortgage, so I never had much extra cash. Which is why when I accepted the job as Hilltop's chef, I decided to bank every penny of my salary."

Erica mentally calculated the sum while swallowing another sip of wine.

"This is the first time in my life I consider myself financially independent." Millie reclined her chair a notch. "Now, if I get a hankering to invite a lonely old codger to share my bed, it won't be because I need his money."

Erica nearly choked.

Amanda laughed. "You're one in a million, Millie."

"Two million." Their chef lifted her wine glass off the end table and swallowed a sip. "Given my culinary skills, I'd be a doggone good catch."

Amanda grabbed a truffle. "Do you already have some unsuspecting old codger in mind?"

"Not yet, and maybe never."

Following another hour of fun conversation and polishing off their wine, Erica and Amanda helped Millie clean up her kitchen before donning their coats and bidding their hostess good night. Outside, Erica breathed in the crisp night air as they headed across the sidewalk and down to the street. "Do you suppose Millie was serious about her old codger comment?"

"All I know is, witnessing her reel in some old guy would be more fun than binge-watching a favorite sitcom."

Images emerged of Millie luring a bearded, old man into her bedroom with snickerdoodles and chocolate cake. Erica chuckled. "As long as she keeps intimate details private."

"No kidding."

They strode past their inn ablaze in lights atop the hill. "Never in my wildest imagination would I have envisioned transforming a rundown mansion into a successful tourist destination."

Amanda looped her arm around Erica's elbow. "Morgan, Wendy, and I had to drive from New Orleans to Asheville to coax you into going along with our plan."

"If Abby hadn't found the courage to face the friends who bullied her, the two of us would be struggling to make ends meet in some dingy Asheville apartment."

"I had no intention of leaving my hometown until Morgan made me admit that I wanted to become financially independent and control my own destiny. Going back to work as a New Orleans tour guide would never have made either possible."

"We owe a lot to our daughters."

"Indeed we do." After entering their kitchen, Erica slipped out of her coat. "I don't know about you, but I'm talked out and ready to call it a night."

"That makes two of us." Amanda filled a glass with water then headed out of the kitchen. "I'll see you tomorrow morning."

Erica followed her through the den. "Sleep well."

Amanda waved over her shoulder as she headed toward her room. "You too."

Erica lifted her laptop off the dining room table then tiptoed to the end of the hall. She opened her daughter's bedroom door a crack and peeked in. Abby was asleep, her wheelchair positioned beside her bed. Dusty lifted her head off the doggie bed and slapped her tail on the floor signaling all was well. Erica pulled the door closed then backtracked to her room between Amanda's private space and the now empty fourth bedroom.

After closing the door, she turned on the bedside lamp and peered at random furniture from her Asheville home's guest rooms—pieces that hadn't sold during their last-minute estate sale. Funny how things worked out.

Erica sat on the side of the bed, balanced her laptop on her thighs, and opened to the blank spreadsheet. Comments Millie and Amanda had made during the evening played in her mind. Both women knew what they wanted. Her fingers hovered over the keyboard. The time had come to stop procrastinating. Erica tapped the keypad then closed the file and set her laptop on her nightstand. After changing into pajamas and turning out the light, she climbed into bed. A moment of doubt niggled her brain. Had she made the right decision, or was there another reason why she wasn't ready to accept Brad's proposal?

Chapter 13

Following five minutes of indecision, Amanda donned a royal blue pantsuit, three-inch heels, and gold loop earrings. Confident she'd made the right choice, she grabbed her purse then walked out of her bedroom and headed to the den.

Humming, Awesam's CEO sat at the dining room table with her laptop open. "You're extra cheery this morning."

"Last night I decided what I need to do." Erica explained. "I'm working out the details now." She glanced up. "You're all dressed up."

Amanda shrugged. "If I'm fifteen minutes away from dealing with bad news, at least I'll look professional."

"I talked to Wendy a few minutes ago."

"Did she mention my meeting with her father-in-law?"

"Not a word. She'll come over after lunch to welcome our twelve bridge-playing guests." Erica tapped her keyboard. "None of those ladies scheduled a massage; however, a local booked a three o'clock for today. That's the third non-guest appointment this year."

"Your reputation as a massage expert is expanding."

"Definitely good for business."

Amanda glanced at her watch. "Time to find out why Keith wants to meet me."

"Call me as soon as you have a chance."

"I will." Amanda grabbed keys off the kitchen counter then headed out the back door and climbed into the truck—the only remaining vehicle connected to Gunter. She backed down to the street and drove to town. A block from her destination, her pulse quickened. The last time she had stepped foot in the Armstrong law office, freelance journalist Gail Weston interviewed her and her partners about Gunter. Days later they approved the article she'd written about their triumph over tragedy. Amanda pulled into the parking lot fronting the single-story building. Time to find out if today was also about the con man.

Amanda breathed deeply then climbed out and strode into the tastefully decorated reception area. Rosalie, the plump, middle-aged receptionist who had served as one of the judges for Hilltop Inn's first annual Holiday Dessert Competition smiled. "Welcome. It's nice to see you again. Is Millie enjoying her reputation as an award-winning chef?"

"Immensely." Did Rosalie have a clue why her boss had arranged this meeting? "How's life treating you?"

"Couldn't be better. Mr. Armstrong is ready for you." Rosalie escorted Amanda past the conference room. She knocked then opened a door. "Ms. Smith is here."

"Show her in."

Amanda stepped into Keith Armstrong's office.

The senior partner stood. "Thank you for agreeing to meet with me."

Was his smile a good sign? "You're welcome."

He motioned to one of two leather armchairs beside a bookcase full of matching law books. "Please have a seat."

Amanda complied. "How's Linda?"

"She's busy with her charity work and enjoying her grandbabies." Keith lowered to his executive chair. "How's everything going at Hilltop?"

"Better than we imagined."

"You ladies manage a first-class inn."

Did he begin every meeting with social pleasantries before delivering bad news? "Thanks to advice from our friend Faith over at Blue Ridge Inn."

Keith scooted his chair closer to the desk. "You know I'm running to replace Richard Watson."

Amanda nodded. "The district attorney who brought a trumped-up charge of reckless endangerment against Jimmy Barkley."

"Whom my son soundly defeated during Jimmy's trial."

"Chris also did an excellent job preparing Wendy, Erica, and me to face Gunter in his Las Vegas murder trial."

"He's an excellent attorney, which brings me to the reason for today's meeting."

Amanda's back stiffened.

Keith scooted his chair closer to his desk. "I want to hire you as my campaign manager."

Amanda blinked. Had she heard him correctly?

"I understand this comes as a surprise."

"More like a shock. Especially since I don't have any political experience."

"Neither do I." Keith crossed his arms on his desk. "However, I'm wise enough to know that I need a manager I can trust—someone who doesn't have deep ties to the community."

Amanda's brows raised. "You mean an outsider who's capable of making objective decisions?"

Keith nodded. "Who's also a smart, no-nonsense business woman who thrives on overcoming challenges."

"Thank you for the compliment." Amanda broke eye contact and peered at the rows of law books. Would becoming involved in a political campaign negatively impact Awesam's reputation? How high a learning curve would she encounter?

"In case you're wondering, Linda and Chris agree you're our best choice."

Did Wendy know about the offer?

"With the election ten months away, we'll have plenty of time to create a winning strategy."

Images of the district attorney's smug attitude during Jimmy Bradley's trial flashed in Amanda's mind. The way he attempted to manipulate the jury with fake southern charm pegged him as a con artist. Amanda faced Keith. "I have to admit, defeating Watson is appealing."

"Are you accepting my offer?"

"When I walked into your office, I half expected to deal with more of Gunter Benson's shenanigans."

"I understand if you need a few days to decide."

Amanda's focus drifted to the landscape painting above the credenza behind Keith's desk. Her role as Awesam's president didn't take all that much time, and Keith was right about her ability to face challenges head-on. Her eyes met his. "I don't need more time."

"What's the verdict?"

Amanda squared her shoulders. "I'd be honored to partner with this area's next district attorney."

A wide smile lit Keith's face. "Welcome aboard, Amanda."

"Thank you. When do you want to meet for our first strategy session?"

"Sunday afternoon at my house."

"I'll be there with a page full of questions and a few ideas."

Keith chuckled. "DA Watson has no idea what he's about to face."

"It will be a pleasure defeating him."

"Indeed it will."

Five minutes after accepting the offer, Amanda returned to the truck and tapped Erica's number. "You won't believe why Keith wanted to meet with me."

Eager for an update, Wendy parked behind the truck then dashed through the kitchen and into the den. Amanda sat at the dining room table with her laptop open. Erica sat across from her. "Did you accept Keith's offer?"

Amanda's brows raised. "You knew?"

"Of course, I knew. I'm married to his son who's also his law partner. I promised not to say anything until after the meeting." Wendy settled between her partners. "You told him yes, didn't you?"

"A little more than an hour ago, I entered the crazy world of politics."

Wendy snapped her fingers. "That crooked DA has no idea what he's up against."

"Your father-in-law made the same comment."

"Because he knows how tough you are."

"I have a lot to learn between now and Sunday." Amanda tapped her keyboard. "Beginning with a political campaign manager's job description."

"Have you told Millie about your new role?"

Amanda shook her head. "I'll break the news tomorrow."

Wendy plucked the inn's ringing phone off the table and swiped her fingers across the screen. "May I help you?"

"Our bridge club members are all here and ready to check in."

"I'm on my way over." Wendy pocketed the phone then headed to the kitchen.

Erica followed her. "I'll go with you."

"Thanks." Wendy grabbed the inn key off the counter then headed out the back door.

Lively female chatter drifted from the front as they rushed past two parked SUVs. "They're a talkative bunch."

Erica nodded. "We're about to experience some of the most fascinating guests thus far."

Wendy's brow pinched. "Meaning what?"

"You'll see."

Curiosity consumed Wendy as they headed up the sidewalk fronting the inn. Why would Erica call a group of bridge-playing ladies fascinating? She climbed onto the porch and summoned her warmest smile. "Welcome to Blue Ridge Inn."

Twelve well-dressed ladies, who all appeared to be sixty-plus, stopped talking and turned in their direction.

"I'm Wendy."

"And I'm Erica. We're delighted you've chosen to stay with us."

A silver-haired woman stepped forward. "I'm Doris, president of the South Carolina Bridge Gals." Her thick accent made it clear she was an honest-to-goodness southerner. "Every year we select a new location to celebrate our friendship and compete in a bragging-rights tournament."

Wendy unlocked the door and held it open. Chatter resumed as the ladies pulled their luggage into the foyer and took in the view.

Bernie rushed in from the back. "We're all ready for you." She pointed to a pair of card tables and eight chairs in the living room. "The third table is set up in our den."

Erica closed the front door. "Since you're our only guests, we arranged the beverages you requested in the dining room."

Doris nodded. "Thank you for taking such good care of us. We'll begin our tournament tomorrow after breakfast. Tonight we'll explore downtown Blue Ridge."

Up to this point, their new guests seemed normal. Wendy moved to the desk. "We'd like you to sign our guest book before we show you to your rooms."

Doris stepped up first, followed by the others. Twenty minutes later Wendy escorted the last two guests to their suite. "Please let us know anything we can do to make your stay special."

"Thank you."

Wendy pulled the door closed then headed down to the foyer. "I have no idea why you find twelve sweet, little old bridge-playing ladies so fascinating."

Erica grinned. "Believe me. Fun is a lot higher on their agenda than cards."

"Because they're friendly?"

"Not exactly."

Wendy followed Erica to the dining room then burst out laughing. A dozen bottles of adult-beverages and an array of appropriate glassware lined up on the sideboard. "No wonder they reserved our dining room for private dinners tomorrow and the next night."

Bernie ambled in from the kitchen "The ladies also requested a lot of fancy snacks to go along with their libations." She placed a stack of clear plastic plates on the sideboard. "Millie's on her way over to begin preparations."

Wendy's eyes widened. "Are they planning to drive to town after cocktails?"

Erica shook her head. "We arranged for two limos to drive them to and from town."

Bernie giggled. "I can't wait to see how Millie interacts with twelve tipsy, card-playing senior citizens."

Wendy lifted a bottle off the sideboard and fingered the label. "I'm definitely coming back tomorrow."

Twenty-three hours after leaving Hilltop Inn, Wendy carried Ryan into the ranch house. "Any word from next door?"

Amanda pushed her laptop aside. "I've been too busy preparing for Sunday's meeting with your father-in-law to ask." She lifted off the dining room chair.

"I appreciate you agreeing to babysit for a couple of hours." Wendy placed her son in his nana's arms.

"I'll always find time to love on my grandson." Amanda carried Ryan to the sofa and plucked a children's book off the coffee table. "We'll have lots of fun while your mommy goes to work."

Ryan babbled while Dusty padded over and plopped her head on the cushion beside Amanda.

"Is Erica keeping an eye on Millie and our guests?"

"She was, until a resident scheduled a last-minute massage."

"That means our guests are alone with Millie and Bernie." Wendy slid the diaper bag off her shoulder and set it on the floor beside the sofa then scooted through the kitchen and out the back door. She raced to the inn's patio and unlocked the sliding glass doors. Inside the den, four ladies sat around a card table. Doris carried on a conversation with the woman sitting across from her while their opponents focused on their cards. So much for a serious tournament.

Wendy smiled when Doris turned toward her. "I hope you ladies are enjoying your stay."

"We're having a delightful time."

"Excellent." Chatter drifted from the living room as Wendy followed cheese and bacon aromas to the kitchen. "What are you baking?"

"Miniature quiches." Millie placed pita bread wedges on a large wooden board arranged with assorted meats, cheeses, and veggies.

"Fancy charcuterie board."

Millie added grapes to the mix. "If you ask me, that's a highfalutin name for a meat and cheese platter."

Bernie arranged miniature sandwiches on a tray. "Not for ladies who are as sophisticated as our guests."

Wendy climbed onto an island stool. No way she'd admit she hadn't a clue about the name until Chris's mom enlightened her. "What have you two learned about our card-playing party guests?"

"Are you suggesting Bernie and I have been snooping on these ladies?"

"I'm way beyond suggesting."

"Since you're one of Hilltop's innkeepers, I'll clue you in." Millie pushed the charcuterie board aside, then closed the door to the dining room then the door to the den. "Five of the ladies are married, three of them happily. Four are divorced and three are widows. One of the widows has reconnected with a guy she dated back in high school. Doris and her husband sold their business for a fortune. She paid for all the booze. Frances is her best friend and married to a retired judge. Two of the ladies inherited bundles from their wealthy families. One is a retired English teacher, and another was a top-selling real estate agent. She still dabbles in the business."

Wendy stared wide-eyed at Millie. "Did you two spend the last six hours interrogating our guests?"

"We didn't need to. They all talk a blue streak, so all we had to do was keep the kitchen doors open and listen." Bernie added a garnish to the sandwich plate. "The oldest lady was a decorated police detective who solved a six-year-old cold case. Would you believe she never goes anywhere without her gun?"

"At this point, I'd believe anything."

Erica ambled in from the den and settled beside Wendy. "Based on your expression, I'm guessing Millie and Bernie have been giving you an earful about our twelve southern-born-and-bred guests."

Wendy failed to swallow a giggle. "Big time."

"Bernie and I agree on one fact."

Wendy smirked. "That you two could give Vincent Adams serious competition?"

Bernie raised a brow. "Who's Vincent Adams?"

"Armstrong law firm's private investigator who tracked down my mother."

"You're right, but that's beside the point." Responding to the timer's ding, Millie removed a pan of mini quiches from the oven. "Bernie and I agreed that if those twelve ladies all lived in Blue Ridge, we'd learn how to play bridge so we could join their club."

Erica chuckled. "Why don't you and Bernie start your own club?"

"Hmm." Millie tapped her finger to her chin. "A Jessica Fletcher mystery club would be a hoot."

Wendy's brows pinched. "Is she one of our guests?"

Their chef stared at Wendy as if she'd grown a third eye. "You've never watched *Murder, She Wrote*?"

Erica slid off her stool. "You realize Wendy wasn't born when that program aired."

"Doesn't matter. She could've watched reruns."

Wendy pulled her phone from her pocket and tapped the screen. "The main character was a mystery writer and an amateur detective." She caught Millie's eye. "A Jessica Fletcher club would be perfect for you two."

Bernie's head tilted. "Some sort of mystery club is a novel idea."

"You two can decide what to do another day." Erica glanced at her watch. In ten minutes our guests' designated cocktail hour begins." She carried the charcuterie board to the dining room. Bernie followed with the sandwiches while Millie transferred the quiches to a platter.

Wendy pocketed her phone. "How do you suppose our guests will act after they start drinking?"

"Like genteel southern ladies who know how to behave while enjoying a rollicking good time."

Wendy laughed. "I can't wait to watch genteel meets rollicking in action."

Chapter 14

An hour after helping Millie and Bernie serve the South Carolina Bridge Gals a gourmet dinner, Erica returned to the ranch house and plopped onto the sofa beside Amanda.

"How'd dinner go?"

"If half of my customers had been as much fun as our guests, all those years I waited tables would have been a lot less stressful."

"How tipsy are the ladies?"

"Enough to have a ball, but not enough to abandon proper southern behavior."

"Are you saying Millie's description of genteel and rollicking is accurate?"

Erica kicked off her shoes and propped her feet on the coffee table. "Tomorrow night you should take my place and decide if her definition is accurate."

"Why not." Amanda closed her book. "I can't think of a more entertaining way to spend the evening before my first planning session with Keith."

"I'm glad you're accepting the challenge to defeat DA Watson."

Amanda shrugged. "Who knows? I might end up enjoying politics."

Abby wheeled in from the hall. Dusty padded behind her. "Has Amanda told you the good news?"

Erica's pulse accelerated. Had her daughter's physical therapist finally given her a positive prognosis? "What news?"

Abby's face beamed. "The crisis center agreed to my suggestion for a full-time comfort dog. The trainer's bringing him over tomorrow. He's a golden like Dusty. His name is Lucky."

Struggling to mask her disappointment, Erica forced a smile. "Lucky is the perfect name for an emotional support animal."

"I agree. About tomorrow, Tommy's dad wants him at the construction site early, so I'll need you to drive me to work. Tommy will pick me up after work and bring me home."

Amanda set her book on the end table. "Now that you two have tomorrow's transportation worked out, what do you say the three of us watch a chick flick."

"Cool. You and Mom pick."

"All right." Amanda ambled to the built-in bookcase beside the fireplace and ran her finger along the shelf displaying their DVD's. "How about *Sweet Home Alabama*?"

Abby rolled her eyes while maneuvering onto the sofa beside Erica. "One of these days, we need to add some movies from the current decade to our collection. Although that is one of my favorites."

"We have a winner." Amanda turned on the television then slid the DVD into the player and returned to the sofa.

Erica scooted closer to Abby, closed her eyes, and sent up a silent prayer for a miracle to touch her daughter.

An hour before the sun crept over the horizon, Erica stepped aside to make room for Abby to steer her wheelchair into the kitchen. "You're extra cheery this morning."

Abby stopped humming. "The kids at the crisis center are excited about today. Especially Sophie. When she came in with her battered mother two days ago, she had the saddest four-year-old eyes I've ever seen. When I told her about Lucky, a little of the sadness seemed to disappear." Abby pulled an orange juice carton from the fridge. "Then before I left yesterday, she hugged me."

"What a sweet moment."

"Helping kids navigate difficult domestic situations is one of the many reasons I love my job."

"The center's director was smart to hire you, sweetheart."

"Same thing she said." Abby downed a glass of orange juice and gobbled a protein bar. "I'll be ready to leave as soon as I brush my teeth."

"I'll move your car."

"Thanks, Mom."

Erica donned a jacket, grabbed the keys from the bowl, and headed out to the carport. Following the familiar routine, she slid behind the steering wheel and backed beside the front sidewalk. After setting the brake and opening the passenger door she headed straight to the front porch.

"Perfect timing." Abby wheeled out the door, down the sidewalk, and onto the driveway.

Erica followed her to the passenger side. After Abby lifted her body onto the seat, Erica folded her child's wheelchair and stashed it in the trunk. Her heart ached as she slid behind the wheel and backed onto the street. Would Abby ever be able to drive her own car? Erica swallowed the lump rising in her throat and forced a smile. "The sun will be up by the time we arrive at the center."

"Do you have time to stay and meet Lucky?"

"Absolutely."

"Cool."

During the remainder of the drive, Abby tapped her phone while Erica laser focused on driving and keeping an eye out for deer. By the time she turned onto the crisis center parking lot, her shoulders ached. "We're here."

Abby pocketed her phone.

Erica hastened to lift the wheelchair from the trunk and roll it to the passenger door.

"Thanks, Mom."

Abby maneuvered onto her chair then wheeled up the ramp to the front door and entered a number on the keypad. The lock clicked. Erica pushed the door open. Abby rolled through the reception area and down a hall. She stopped beside an open door. "Good morning."

Erica followed her daughter into the cozy gathering room. A young woman with a black eye and a cut lip sat on the sofa. An adorable curly-haired little girl clutching a stuffed bear to her chest climbed off her mother's lap and rushed to Abby. "Where's Lucky?"

"He's on his way. Mom, meet my new friend Sophie."

Erica stooped and smiled. "It's a pleasure to meet you, Sophie."

The child's chin dipped to her chest.

Her mother scooted to the edge of the sofa. "My daughter is shy around strangers."

Erica's eyes focused on the child. "Know what? So am I. But now you and I are no longer strangers, are we?"

Sophie shook her head.

"What's your bear's name?"

The child peered up at Erica. "Fuzzy."

"What a perfect name for your furry friend."

"My daddy gave it to me for my birthday. We can't live with him anymore because he hurts Mommy."

Erica's heart ached. She knew all too well the trauma the little girl and her mother were experiencing. The front door intercom buzzed. Erica smiled. "Guess what? I bet Lucky's here."

Abby reached out to Sophie. "Do you want to ride with me?"

"Uh-huh." The child's eyes brightened as she climbed onto Abby's lap. "We'll go nice and slow."

Erica followed her daughter to the front door.

Abby pressed the intercom. "May I help you?"

"I'm John, here with Lucky."

Abby unlocked the door. "Come on in."

Seconds after the door opened, the golden retriever bounded in, his tail setting his backside in motion. Sophie squealed with delight as the crisis center's new resident's tongue bathed her cheek.

His trainer followed. "Heel, Lucky."

Sophie's new canine pal sat on his haunches and peered up at his trainer.

John patted the dog's head. "Good boy." Lucky responded with a tail wag. The young man handed Abby a sheet of paper. "He responds to all of those commands."

"Wow." Abby ran her finger down the list. "He's one smart dog."

"One of the brightest and most lovable I've trained. I'll bring his gear and a week's worth of food in from my truck."

"Thank you."

John handed Abby the leash then walked out. After he delivered the items, Abby led Lucky to the gathering room and introduced him to two more young children who had come in with their mother.

Erica's heart warmed as the little ones giggled and gathered around their new canine friend. She leaned close to Abby. "There's nothing like a sweet dog to bring joy into children's lives." Abby exchanged a knowing look with her, making it clear her daughter understood the depth of her comment.

Fifteen minutes after welcoming Lucky, the front door intercom buzzed. "His trainer must have forgotten something."

Erica followed Abby as she steered her chair to the reception area. She pressed the intercom button. "May I help you?"

No response.

Erica peeked through the peep hole. "I don't see anyone."

"Probably a delivery."

"I'll check." Erica unlocked the door and opened it a crack. A high-pitched, tiny cry emanated from the black gym bag someone had left on the stoop.

Abby wheeled closer. "Did someone give us a kitten?"

"That's a human sound."

Abby gasped.

Erica's heart pounded as she pulled the door open then lifted the bag onto Abby's lap. She opened the zipper. Inside lay an infant with a cleft lip swaddled in a blue blanket. A note lay on the baby's chest. Erica handed the note to Abby then lifted the infant into her arms.

"The note says, '*My baby's name is Theo. I love him with all my heart, but he needs more help than I'm capable of giving. Please find someone to give him the care he deserves.*'"

Erica unwrapped the blanket and eyed the fresh umbilical cord stump. "This child needs to be hospitalized."

"I'll call for an ambulance." Abby pulled her phone from her pocket and tapped the screen.

Erica picked Theo up and rocked the crying infant. "What heartless person would leave a tiny baby on a doorstep in freezing cold weather? I don't want to think about what would have happened if we hadn't heard the buzzer or opened the door."

"God meant for you and me to rescue this child, Mom."

Theo stopped crying. Was finding an abandoned infant God's way of answering her prayer for a miracle in her daughter's life?

Five minutes after Abby placed the phone call, help arrived. EMTs rushed to assess the infant before carrying him to the ambulance. As they drove away, Erica understood deep in her soul that she and Abby hadn't seen the last of the abandoned child.

Moments after Erica placed their supper plates in the dishwasher, she grabbed her ringing phone off the dining room table. "Hey, Millie. Is everything okay?"

"One of your guests wants you and Abby to come over now."

"Which guest and why?"

"Dorothy. To talk about the baby you rescued."

Abby wheeled in from the kitchen. "What's up?"

Erica placed her hand over the phone. "Seems Millie is equally adept at leaking and gathering information."

"I heard that." Millie's tone hinted of irritation. "Are you coming or not?"

Erica sighed. "Tell Dorothy we're on the way."

Abby's head tilted. "Who are we meeting?"

Erica explained while pushing her daughter's chair to Hilltop's back patio. Loud chatter drifted from the dining room as they entered the den.

An attractive elderly woman ambled in from the foyer. "I appreciate you both coming over." Dorothy created a space at the card table for Abby's wheelchair, then motioned toward a chair. "Please."

Erica complied. "What's on your mind?"

Dorothy settled across from Erica. "I believe a desperate mother leaving her newborn for you and your daughter to find is one of those life events orchestrated by a higher power. However, there's another reason I wanted to meet with you." Dorothy laced her fingers on the table. "My husband, God rest his soul, was a renowned plastic surgeon, so I'm familiar with that particular birth defect. If the infant you rescued has a cleft lip and not a cleft palate, surgery should take place within his first few months."

"I appreciate the information." Erica's eyes shifted from their guest to Abby. Was this stranger's reference to the rescue a coincidence or something more profound?

Chapter 15

Amanda parked at the curb in front of Keith and Linda Armstrong's two-story, stone-and-brick house overlooking downtown Blue Ridge. She closed her eyes and gripped the truck's steering wheel as images from the final day of Jimmy Barkley's trial skated through her mind. Moments after the jury foreman announced a not-guilty verdict, DA Watson had slammed his briefcase shut and headed straight to the exit. His contorted expression and clenched fist spoke volumes. The man hated to lose. A knot gripped Amanda's belly. What underhanded tactics would he employ to defeat the candidate determined to replace him?

A shudder skittered up Amanda's spine. Managing a contentious political campaign was riddled with risk, especially in a close-knit community. No matter what shenanigans their opponent tried to pull, she vowed not to cross any lines that would damage her integrity and Hilltop Inn's reputation. Amanda drew in a deep breath. As her racing pulse slowed, she opened her eyes and peeled her fingers off the steering wheel. After shouldering her purse and grabbing her laptop off the passenger seat, she climbed out and made her way up the sidewalk to the front porch. The time had come to follow through on her commitment. She hesitated a moment then pressed the bell.

Linda pulled the front door open. "Welcome back to our home."

"Thank you." Amanda pasted on her best smile and stepped into the house she had last visited to celebrate Thanksgiving with her extended family. "How are your daughter and granddaughter doing?"

Linda's face beamed. "Allison is seeing patients four days a week, and like Ryan, Ellie's more adorable every day. Grandchildren are among life's most precious gifts."

"Indeed they are."

Linda pushed the door closed. "How's life treating your daughter and son-in-law?"

"Morgan and Kevin are scheduled to close on their new home in a few days."

"What an exciting time for them. Will they live close to the city?"

Amanda shook her head. "A suburb about twenty miles north of downtown Atlanta."

"We're blessed that our children married well. Enough about family. I imagine you're eager to begin working on Keith's campaign."

Anxious more accurately described Amanda's state of mind.

"Keith and Gary are downstairs relaxing before the big meeting. Gary's a great guy and a close family friend. You'll enjoy working with him."

Amanda's brow pinched then released. Who was Gary, and why hadn't Keith mentioned him? Her chest tightened as she followed Linda down to a large paneled room with a high ceiling. A distinguished-looking man sporting a neatly trimmed salt-and-pepper beard aimed his cue stick and sank the last ball in the corner pocket. Why did he look familiar?

"Amanda's here, darling."

Keith turned toward them, grinning. "Perfect timing, given this pool shark has cheated his way to another victory."

"Attorneys aren't known for losing graciously." Keith's friend stepped around the pool table and extended his hand to Amanda. "I'm Gary Redding." A smile sent a twinkle to his blue eyes. "Keith's campaign finance manager and expert pool player."

Amanda tucked her laptop under her left arm then accepted his hand. "It's a pleasure." He sandwiched her outstretched hand, releasing an unexpected tingling sensation. "We've met before, haven't we?"

"Briefly, during Hilltop Inn's grand opening last May."

Amanda dug deep into her memory bank. What had Millie said about him when she reviewed the guest list Linda had provided? "Of course. You're the president of a local bank, right?"

"Guilty as charged." He released Amanda's hand.

Keith clapped his friend's shoulder. "One reason he's a financial genius."

Gary's eyes remained focused on Amanda. "My pal is flattering me because I agreed to manage his campaign for free. Actually, I owe him for expert legal representation a few years back. That's another story for another day."

His easy-going manner and charm helped ease Amanda's anxiety, especially since she wouldn't be responsible for managing the campaign's money.

Keith lifted his hand off his friend's shoulder. "Now that we're all here, we'll jump right into our kick-off meeting."

Linda nudged Amanda. "I'm the campaign secretary, otherwise known as the volunteer notetaker."

Keith winked at his wife. "Who's also gorgeous and brilliant."

"After all these years, flattery still works." Linda patted her husband's cheek. "Along with your promise to cook dinner every Saturday night until after the election."

"I ended up with the better part of that deal."

Linda grinned. "Definitely."

Keith swept his arm toward a round pedestal table beside a window overlooking the patio beneath the deck. "Welcome to the campaign conference center."

Amanda settled on a high-back leather chair between the men and across from Linda, then added her laptop to the three already placed on the table.

"Before we begin—" Keith's focus shifted from Linda to Gary, then to Amanda. "I want you all to know how much I appreciate you joining my team and helping me defeat Richard Watson."

"I understand the personal and financial sacrifices you're making to bring integrity back to the district attorney's office." Gary scooted his chair closer to the table. "Your father would be proud of you."

Linda touched her husband's arm. "We're all proud of you, darling."

Keith placed his hand over his wife's. "I couldn't do this without your support, sweetheart."

Amanda swallowed the lump rising in her throat. Keith and Linda's devotion to each other reminded her of how much she had lost the day the drunk driver ended Preston's life.

"I'd like to hear from you first, Amanda."

Keith's voice broke through the fog. Amanda blinked. "All right." She opened her laptop and pulled up a document. Two hours after her suggestion began a productive dialogue, she leaned back. "That's all I have."

"My pal was smart to hire you." Gary's eyes met Amanda's. "No one would ever believe this is your first political campaign."

A sensation akin to a flurry of butterflies fluttered in Amanda's chest. What was it about this man that affected her? "I brainstormed ideas with my business partners, so some of the credit belongs to them."

"Surrounding one's self with talented people is a smart political tactic." Keith pushed his laptop aside. "And deserving of dinner at one of our town's finest restaurants. My treat, if you two don't have other plans."

Gary scooted his chair away from the table. "Anytime you're buying, I'm on board. What about you, Amanda? Are you free to join us?"

"I am. However, given Keith hasn't announced he's running, we need to avoid discussing anything about the campaign in public."

"A campaign manager's number one responsibility." Gary closed his laptop. "Protect the candidate from idle gossip—a tall order in a small town."

Amanda stole a quick glance at the campaign's finance manager. How much had Keith and Linda told him about her, and why did he owe Keith a favor? Maybe she would learn the answers during dinner.

At half past nine Amanda walked into the ranch house kitchen and tossed the truck keys into the bowl. Dusty greeted her with a tail wag as she ambled into the den.

Erica sat in a club chair with an open book on her lap. "How was the meeting and dinner?"

Amanda dropped onto the chair across from her "The meeting was productive, the dinner interesting."

Erica closed her book. "Two nondescript responses."

Amanda crossed one leg over the other. "Do you remember meeting Gary Redding during Hilltop's open house?"

"We met so many people that night. Maybe if you describe him—"

"Good-looking. Distinguished. Late forties or early fifties. Salt-and-pepper hair and beard."

"Vaguely. Why?"

"Gary is our campaign finance manager. He owes Keith for representing him in a contentious divorce a few years back."

"Contentious how?"

"He didn't explain."

"Hmm."

Amanda stared at her partner, her brow furrowed. "What's with that response?"

Erica set her book on the end table. "Seems you'll spend the next nine months working with a handsome divorced man who obviously impressed you."

Amanda smirked. "What makes you think I'm the least bit impressed?"

Erica shrugged. "The subtle gleam in your eyes when you described him."

"Now you're an expert on my facial expressions?"

"We've lived and worked together for more than a year, so yeah, I recognize the signs."

"No matter what's going on in your brain, Gary is a good addition to Keith's team. Nothing more."

"Until he invites you out to dinner."

Amanda rolled her eyes. "You're delusional."

Erica tilted her head. "Am I?"

"Hopelessly." Amanda shifted her focus to the burning fireplace embers. What if Erica was right, and Gary found her intriguing enough to invite her for dinner or a drink? She rolled her eyes. No point wasting time speculating about something that would likely never happen.

Chapter 16

A half mile from their destination, Erica gripped the steering wheel. Returning to the hospital months after Abby's accident released painful memories. The long hours she'd waited for news about her daughter in the emergency room with Amanda and Wendy. The shock when the neurologist explained Abby's incomplete spinal cord injury. The pain seeing her unconscious child lying in the intensive care unit with a neck brace stabilizing her spine.

Abby reached across the console and touched Erica's arm. "Are you okay, Mom?"

Erica blinked. "I had hoped we wouldn't have to return to the hospital any time soon."

"At least this time neither of us are patients."

"Thank goodness." Erica pulled into the parking lot and drove past a handicap spot. Abby had refused to apply for a handicap permit, claiming her wheelchair was nothing more than a temporary inconvenience. With each new month, Erica's confidence that her child's claim had merit diminished a fraction. She pulled into an empty space and cut the engine. "Are you ready?"

Abby faced the windshield, seemingly staring into space. "What would have happened to Theo if we hadn't heard the doorbell?"

"Except we did hear it because we were meant to find him."

Abby failed to respond.

What images were playing in her daughter's mind? Erica patted her daughter's arm. "My turn to ask if you're okay?"

Abby blinked as if emerging from a fog. "Yeah." She opened her door.

Minutes after climbing from the driver's seat, Erica held the hospital door open for Abby. They headed straight to the reception desk. The volunteer looked up. "May I help you?"

Erica explained the reason for their visit.

The woman tapped a keyboard then peered at a screen. "They're expecting you."

Erica walked beside Abby as they headed toward the nursery. When they arrived, Abby wheeled her chair close to the viewing window. Four of the five bassinets were empty. Theo slept in the fifth.

Abby tapped the glass.

A nurse looked up and nodded. She lifted Theo from his bassinet and carried him out to the hall. "This precious child is lucky you ladies found him."

Erica eyed Theo's blue stocking cap. "How's he doing?"

"Much better now that you're here. Come with me." She led them to an empty patient room. "There's nothing more important to a newborn than human touch. Who wants to hold him first?"

Abby peered up at Erica. "Do you mind if I do?"

"Go ahead, sweetheart."

The nurse placed the swaddled infant in Abby's arms. "Cleft-lip babies require a special feeding technique." She handed Erica a business card. "That's my number. Call me when he cries, and I'll show you how to feed him."

Erica stared at the number. "All right."

The nurse walked out, leaving the door open.

"He's so tiny and helpless." Abby brushed her finger across the baby's cleft lip. "And beautiful. Do you suppose his mother would have abandoned him if he'd been born without a birth defect?"

"I doubt we'll ever know." Erica settled on a rocking chair. She fought to keep tears at bay as Abby began humming and rocking the infant in her arms. What sort of future lay in store for this abandoned child? What about her daughter? Would Abby's injury prevent her from one day having a child of her own?

"I heard you two had arrived." Allison ambled in.

Failing to stop the tears from escaping, Erica swiped her cheeks and peered up at Wendy's sister-in-law. "News travels fast."

Allison's smile hinted that she understood her emotion. "Small town, small hospital."

Erica eyed Allison's scrubs. "I assume you're here as Dr. Baker."

"Good assumption. A half-hour ago, I delivered a beautiful baby girl." Allison sat on the edge of the bed. "Earlier today I spoke to the pediatrician assigned to Theo's case. You'll both be happy to know that you rescued a healthy baby."

Abby's brows raised. "What happens to Theo now?"

"The hospital will coordinate with Child Services to find a suitable foster home."

Erica exchanged a knowing glance with her daughter.

"You're both thinking about Wendy's less than desirable foster-home experiences, aren't you?"

Erica's focus shifted to Allison. "Tragic is a more accurate description."

"Rest assured that any potential foster parents will be carefully screened before Theo is released to their care."

Erica's brows shot up. "The social workers who placed Wendy most likely followed the same procedure, so how can you be sure?"

"Because the woman in charge is a close family friend."

Abby tilted her head. "Finding a good home is only half the problem. How much would closing up Theo's lip cost?"

"Considering cleft lip reconstruction is cosmetic surgery, without insurance I'm guessing north of five grand."

Erica sighed. "That's a lot of money."

Abby peeled the blanket back, releasing Theo's hands. "We'll set up a GoFundMe campaign today."

Allison snapped her fingers. "Great idea. Given Blue Ridge residents' big hearts, I suspect you'll raise enough money to schedule surgery for early spring."

Abby touched the infant's hand. "Did you hear the good news?" Theo's eyes opened. Tears welled and spilled down Abby's cheeks the moment his tiny hand curled around her finger. "Before long—" her voice faltered. "You'll be perfect."

Overwhelmed by love for her daughter, Erica pulled her phone from her purse and snapped photos of Abby cradling the child they had rescued. "Those pictures will tug on heartstrings."

"As well as open wallets." Allison rose. "I'll keep you updated on progress toward finding a foster home for Theo."

Abby peered up at Allison. "He deserves a family who will love him with all their hearts."

"Yes, he does." Allison smiled then walked out.

After devoting two hours to snuggling and feeding the abandoned infant, Erica and Abby returned to the car. They remained silent during the drive, each lost in their own thoughts. Moments after arriving home, Abby headed straight to her room.

Erica returned to the driveway and pulled her daughter's car into the carport. Halfway to the back door, she pulled her ringing phone from her pocket and swiped her finger across the screen. "Hey, Brad."

"How's Theo?"

"Thriving." Erica walked inside and settled on the den sofa while relaying the details. "I hope Allison's confidence in Child Services finding a suitable home isn't a pipe dream."

"Years ago Lauren and Carl fostered a two-year-old girl until the child's mother completed rehab and stayed sober for six months."

Erica's mind drifted to the last time she and Brad played golf with his and his late wife's closest friends. "Did they have a difficult time letting the child go?"

"Especially Lauren. They still stay in touch with the girl and her mother. Anyway, Chris and I have everything planned for tomorrow night."

Erica eyed the still-life painting hanging above the fireplace mantel. "A year ago Wendy, Amanda, and I spent Valentine's Day in Las Vegas testifying at Gunter's murder trial. Which makes this year that much more special."

"Lucky me. Gotta run. A parent just arrived for a conference about her son bullying another kid. I'll pick you up tomorrow at five."

"I'll be ready." Erica set her phone on the end table then leaned back and closed her eyes. Seven and a half months ago, she'd met Brad for the first time at Hilltop Inn's open house, and now his engagement ring was hidden in her dresser drawer. Once she accepted his proposal, how long would their engagement last? When they married would she move into the home he shared with his first love?

Footsteps striking the kitchen floor followed the back door closing.

Erica's eyes popped open.

"Today's arrivals are checked in." Amanda dropped onto the sofa beside Erica. "How'd the hospital visit go?"

"Better than I expected." For the second time, she shared details.

Before Erica finished, Abby wheeled into the den. She stopped on the other side of the coffee table, set her laptop down, and turned the screen toward Erica. "Tell me what you think."

Erica scooted to the edge of the sofa and read the GoFundMe page. "Well done, sweetheart." She slid the laptop to Amanda.

"Brilliant idea. Know what else we should do?" Amanda pushed the laptop back to Abby. "Take Nancy up on her offer for another interview on her podcast. Except this time you'll join us and tell Theo's story."

"Cool."

Erica's focus shifted from Abby to Amanda. "When Nancy invited us to return for another interview, she asked us to bring Millie."

"We'll let the pro work out the details." Amanda pulled her phone from her pocket and tapped the screen. Three minutes later she responded to an incoming text. "We're all set for an interview on Nancy's Nuggets next week."

"The Awesam team comes through again." Abby closed her laptop. "A podcast plus a GoFundMe should raise enough money to make Theo perfect."

"On to another important topic." Amanda leaned back. "How do you and Tommy plan to celebrate Valentine's Day?"

"After we host a party for the mothers and children at the crisis center, we're going out for pizza. What about you?"

"I'm glad you asked." Amanda's tone hinted of humor. "Millie, Bernie, and I will cater to a lovely couple who have chosen to celebrate the holiday with a private dinner in Hilltop's dining room."

Abby's head tilted. "Hopefully, next year you'll celebrate with a guy who's crazy about you."

Amanda raised a brow. "Did your mother tell you about Gary?"

Abby shrugged. "Who?"

Erica thumped Amanda's arm. "You let that kitty out of the litter box, not me."

"Well." Abby grinned. "Whoever this Gary guy is, he's obviously on your mind."

"Only because we're both working on Keith's campaign, and if either of you breathe a word to Millie—"

"Forget about us." Erica laughed. "We all know Millie will find out about him on her own."

Amanda jeered. "Not if I have any say about it."

Chapter 17

An hour before sunset, Amanda pulled her down jacket tight across her chest and traipsed across the side yard to Hilltop's front sidewalk. Although spending time with Millie and Bernie wasn't high on her list of fun ways to spend Valentine evening, at least she wouldn't end up with Dusty as her only companion.

A squirrel eyed her from the porch railing. "Yeah, I know. I'm invading your territory." Amanda rolled her eyes as the critter turned tail and scurried away. "Now I'm talking to rodents." She climbed the stairs and unlocked the door, then followed the lemon and butter aromas to the kitchen. After peeling out of her jacket, she climbed onto a stool and fingered a bottle of Barolo. "Let me guess, the Romanos selected veal piccata."

Millie twisted the lid off a jar of capers. "An Italian meal for an Italian couple, with tiramisu for dessert."

Bernie added bite-sized pieces of romaine to a salad bowl. "We appreciate you helping us tonight."

Amanda shrugged. "I enjoy spending time with you two."

"Who do you think you're kidding?" Millie waggled her finger at Amanda. "You're only here because you're too stubborn to find yourself an eligible man."

"Don't give her a hard time, Millie." Bernie pushed the bowl aside. "Amanda's happy being single."

Millie scoffed. "She's forty-four-years-old. If she spends the next twenty-plus years going to bed alone every night, she'll end up a cranky old lady no one wants around."

"You and I both live alone."

Millie glared at Bernie as if she had lost her mind. "We were already old when our husbands passed on. Amanda was in her early thirties when she became a widow, and her so-called second husband was a scumbag. Although Gunter's the reason this inn exists and we all have jobs."

"Enough already." Amanda drummed her fingers on the island. "In case you haven't noticed, I'm still sitting here."

"Yeah, well." Millie propped her hand on her hip. "If I was your age, gorgeous, and single, you can bet I'd have my picture posted on at least one of those internet dating sites."

"I suggest you forget about playing cupid and focus on the task at hand."

"See?" Millie lowered her hand to her side. "She's already cranky."

"Ugh." Amanda slid off her stool and grabbed the bottle of wine. She waved over her shoulder as she headed toward the dining room. "I'll wait in the living room to greet our guests." She closed the door behind her.

Easy-listening instrumental music floated in the air. Amanda skirted the table surrounded by twelve empty chairs and ambled to the table set for two beside the window. Were Kevin and Morgan dining out tonight? Amanda set the bottle on the table and peered out at the rocking chairs on the front porch. What about Kevin's parents? Were they celebrating at home or in a New Orleans restaurant?

Amanda breathed deeply then slowly released the air and strode into the living room. Gas flames flickering in the fireplace and light from the dimmed chandelier added to the romantic ambiance.

Voices drifted from the foyer. One of the couples she had checked in yesterday descended the stairs and headed to the front door. Where had they reserved their Valentine dinner? Amanda ambled to the scrapbook lying on a bookstand. Her chest puffed as she flipped through pages displaying the home's transformation from a rundown mansion that had remained vacant for more than two decades to an elegant inn. Pausing at a picture of Millie's English country garden under construction, she had to admit the backyard masterpiece was a huge plus for their guests. Her focus drifted to the engraved plaque claiming their chef as the winner of 'Hilltop Inn's Holiday Dessert Competition.' One fact was certain. Life was never dull with Millie around.

Amanda turned toward footsteps striking the foyer floor. A couple who appeared to be in their late sixties or early seventies strolled into the living room holding hands. "Mr. and Mrs. Romano?"

The gentleman grinned. "In the flesh."

Mrs. Romano smiled. "We wanted to relax in this lovely room while waiting for our reserved time."

Her husband escorted her to the sofa.

Amanda ambled over. "May I pour you each a glass of wine?"

Mrs. Romano peered up at Amanda. "I'd love a pre-dinner drink. What about you, honey?"

He held up two fingers.

After returning to the dining room and pulling the cork from the bottle, Amanda returned to the living room and handed each guest a wineglass. "We're delighted you're celebrating Valentine's Day with us."

"We're celebrating far more than a Hallmark holiday." Mr. Romano clicked his glass to his wife's. "A week ago my bride of forty-eight years celebrated five years as cancer free."

"What wonderful news." Amanda pressed her hand to her chest. "Congratulations."

"A lot of prayer, good doctors, and my sweet husband gave me the strength to fight and win the battle."

The couple's eyes met as he slid his arm around his wife's shoulders. "Following her first positive report, we vowed to cherish every moment we have together."

Mrs. Romano patted his knee. "We created a bucket list, like the movie. Except my husband is a lot more handsome than Jack Nicholson."

Amanda struggled to swallow the lump forming in her throat. If either Preston or the drunk driver had stayed home that fateful day, she would be celebrating the twenty-sixth Valentine's Day with the love of her life.

Mrs. Romano peered up at Amanda. "I hope you have someone as special as my sweet husband to help you celebrate."

No way she'd allow out-of-control emotions spoil the moment for her guests. Amanda summoned a smile. "I'm blessed with a loving family and friends. Plus, as one of Hilltop's innkeepers, I have the opportunity to meet so many wonderful couples like you."

Mrs. Romano lifted her hand off her husband's knee. "I imagine you lead an exciting life."

She had no idea. "I can honestly say there's rarely a dull moment. I'll leave you to enjoy your wine while I check on your dinner."

"Thank you for making the evening special for my wife and me."

"We're here to serve you and make Hilltop Inn your home away from home." Amanda made it to the foyer before she lost the battle to keep her emotions at bay. She stepped into the powder room and dabbed her cheeks with a tissue. In twenty years would people refer to her as the cranky old lady who slept alone every night? Ridiculous. A lot of single women led productive, satisfying lives. Counting on Millie being too busy to notice her reddened eyes, Amanda squared her shoulders and returned to the kitchen. "Our dinner guests are enjoying a glass of wine in the living room." She breathed in the sweet and savory aromas. "What smells so delicious?"

"Bacon-wrapped dates with goat cheese." Millie removed a pan from the oven then transferred the dates to a plate. "My new appetizer."

Amanda climbed onto a stool. "When did you add appetizers to the menu?"

"Yesterday." Millie transferred six dates secured with toothpicks to a plate, leaving three on the pan. "They're on the house tonight. If they're a hit, I'll price them out and add them to our menu options." Millie carried the plate out of the kitchen.

Bernie grated fresh parmesan onto the plated Caesar salads. "I didn't want to say anything in front of Millie, but your eyes give you away."

Afraid her emotions were still too raw, Amanda plucked a date off the pan and tasted it. "Oh my gosh, this is delicious."

"You don't have to pretend with me. I've teared up every holiday since my husband passed on to our eternal home."

"Preston and I enjoyed fourteen wonderful years in our little shotgun house. When I returned to New Orleans for my daughter's wedding, Morgan and I drove to our old neighborhood. Every house on our block had been demolished to make way for condos." Amanda's voice faltered. "Now all I have are memories of our life together."

Bernie leaned across the island and placed her hand on Amanda's arm. "You need to hold onto those memories, honey, without allowing them to rob you of your future happiness."

The compassion in Bernie's eyes reached in and touched Amanda's soul.

Millie breezed in. "Mr. and Mrs. Romano are the perfect Valentine couple." She stared at Amanda. "They told you their story, didn't they?"

Grateful their guests provided a logical explanation for her tears, she nodded then swiped her fingers across her cheeks. The moment her eyes met Bernie's, Amanda knew her friend wouldn't reveal the true reason for her emotional response.

After tucking her sleepy-eyed little guy into his crib and kissing his cheek, Wendy pulled his bedroom door closed then returned to the great room. Instrumental music, candles, and a crackling fire created a deliciously romantic setting. Wendy laced her fingers around Chris's neck and breathed in the intoxicating scent of his cologne. "You've gone all out to make tonight special."

He wrapped his arms around Wendy's waist and pulled her close. "You look especially beautiful tonight."

She tilted her head. "Enjoying dinner at home is the perfect way to celebrate. Especially since you and your former coach are doing all the work."

"Our way of showing you both how special you are."

"Hopefully tonight will move Erica one step closer to taking Brad's ring box out of her dresser drawer. By the way, she doesn't know I shared her secret with you."

Chris winked. "What secret?"

Duke abandoned his spot beside the fireplace and raced to the front door.

"Seems our guests have arrived." Chris released Wendy. "Why don't you greet them while I open a bottle of wine."

"Great idea." She unlaced her fingers then headed to the entrance. Duke's tail wag set his backside in motion as Wendy pulled the door open.

After hastening to the passenger door and holding Erica's hand as she stepped out of his Corvette, Brad removed a covered container from the trunk. He pressed his hand to Erica's back as they climbed onto the porch and stepped inside. "Thank you for sharing Valentine's Day with us."

Wendy pushed the door closed once they'd entered. "We're delighted you and Erica are celebrating with us." She tapped her finger on the container. "What did you bring?"

Brad grinned. "Almost homemade brownies with fudge icing."

"The perfect dessert." Wendy's eyes met Erica's, hoping she'd take the hint. "Our guys are going all out to make tonight special for us."

After setting the dessert on the kitchen counter and helping Erica out of her coat, Brad clasped his hand on Chris's shoulder. "I'm ready to go to work, Counselor."

Chris removed two glass baking dishes from the fridge, releasing mouth-watering rosemary, garlic, and balsamic aromas.

Erica sniffed. "Those steaks smell delicious."

"Thanks to my sister's marinade recipe." Chris gave the dishes to Brad then handed Wendy and Erica glasses of wine. "You ladies relax while Coach and I head out to the deck to prepare our Valentine feast."

Wendy draped Erica's coat over a stool. "Don't worry about our guys freezing. We have a ginormous heater to keep them toasty warm."

Duke followed Chris and Brad outside while Wendy and Erica settled on the sofa in front of the fireplace.

Erica leaned back. "Know what would make tonight even more special?"

Wendy splayed her left hand and wiggled her ring finger. "You showing up wearing your engagement ring?"

"Not until I'm ready."

"If not the ring, what?"

"Amanda and a date celebrating with us."

"Hmm." Wendy crossed one leg over the other and pumped her foot. Should she or shouldn't she share what she knew?

Erica tapped her arm. "You might as well admit you're dying to tell me something important."

Linda hadn't sworn her to secrecy, so why not enlighten Erica? "All right, here goes." Wendy stilled her foot and faced Erica. "Has Amanda told you about Gary Redding?"

"Yeah. He's the bank president and Keith's campaign finance manager."

"Oh, he's way more." Wendy leaned close to Erica as if she was seconds from divulging a delicious bit of news. "Gary Redding is one half of Linda's secret plan."

Erica stared wide-eyed at Wendy. "Are you suggesting Chris's mother is playing Cupid?"

"Stating, not suggesting. Seems my mother-in-law believes Amanda is the perfect woman for Gary."

"Are you serious?"

Wendy nodded. "As a matchmaker hoping to collect a big fat fee."

"Does Gary have the slightest idea what she's up to?"

"He's a guy—"

"So he doesn't have a clue."

Wendy snapped her fingers. "Bingo."

"What about Keith?" Erica raised a brow. "Does he approve of his wife playing matchmaker?"

"Linda's a strong-willed woman, and he's crazy about her. What do you think?"

"He's going along with her plan."

"Good guess." Wendy sipped her wine. "According to Chris, Gary and Amanda are a great match."

"How long do you suppose it'll be before Amanda figures out she's the target of Cupid's arrow?"

"Are you kidding? Given how resistant Amanda is to the idea of dating, she's likely to remain oblivious." Wendy paused. "Although, despite her stubborn streak, she deserves to find love again. That's why we need to help Linda's plan work. Subtly, of course."

"What devious tactics are brewing in your cheerleader brain?"

"Well." Wendy tapped her finger to her chin. "Who bugs Amanda the most about finding a man?"

Her partner gawked at Wendy as if she'd grown a third eye. "You're not seriously considering including Millie, are you?"

Wendy shrugged. "Why not?"

"How many reasons do you need?"

"I know the idea might sound crazy—"

"Might?" Erica's eyes remained laser focused on Wendy. "You've already decided, haven't you?"

Wendy picked at a fingernail. "Don't you believe Amanda's future happiness is worth the risk?"

"We're not a couple of teenagers attempting to start a romance between our girlfriend and the captain of the football team."

Wendy huffed. "A simple yes or no will do."

"Does my opinion really matter?"

"Actually—" Wendy hesitated. "Except for serious issues, our Awesam team accepts a majority decision. Given Amanda can't cast a vote on a plan she's not supposed to know about, and you and I cancel each other, Millie would be the tiebreaker."

A bemused grin curled Erica's lips. "Although I'm not changing my vote, it makes sense in a convoluted way."

Wendy tilted her head. "That's why I'll talk to Millie before Monday's board meeting. For now, let's focus on how blessed we are to have two wonderful men in our lives."

Chapter 18

Monday morning Wendy carried Ryan into their home office and lowered him into his playpen. "Daddy's gonna take care of you while Mommy goes to Awesam's monthly board meeting. But first, I need to talk to your daddy."

Chris pushed his chair away from his desk and peered up at Wendy. "You're ready to tell me what you and Erica are cooking up, aren't you?"

"How'd you know? Oh yeah—" Wendy rolled her eyes. "You're an expert at reading people."

"Yup."

"Okay, here's what's going on." Wendy moved her chair beside his then relayed her Valentine's Day conversation with Erica. "What's your opinion, given you're my husband and an attorney?"

"Are you planning to break any laws?"

"Not that I know of."

"In that case—" Chris patted Wendy's knee. "I'm smart enough to stay out of your way."

"All right, then." Wendy kissed his cheek then stood and grabbed her purse off the desk. Halfway to the door, she halted and glanced over her shoulder. "One more thing. Does Gary know about your mom's plan?"

"Not unless he figured it out on his own."

Confident she had made the right decision, Wendy squared her shoulders and headed straight to the garage. During the short drive, she hummed along to a country CD. Funny how country music had become her favorite.

When she arrived at the ranch house, Wendy stopped humming. Time to put step two into action. She eased up the driveway and parked behind the truck. When would Amanda and Erica trade the last physical reminder of Gunter in on a new car? She released a sigh, then climbed out. Hoping no one would see her, Wendy eased into the kitchen and lifted an inn key from the bowl on the counter. Relieved neither of her partners were in sight, she slipped out and rushed across the side yard to Hilltop's front porch. Inside, Wendy greeted a couple sipping coffee in the living room then moved on to the kitchen. Mouthwatering chocolate and brown sugar scents floated in the air. "Are you baking cookies?"

Millie peered over her shoulder. "Don't I always bring a snack to our staff meetings?"

"Yeah, you do."

"There's your answer." Millie removed a baking sheet from the oven and set it on a cooling rack. "Are you here to discuss my new appetizer menu?"

"What are you talking about?"

"Obviously not." Millie skirted the island and climbed onto a stool. "You didn't come all the way over here to chitchat, did you?"

"Not exactly." Wendy settled beside Millie. "What has Amanda told you about her role as Keith Armstrong's campaign manager?"

"Not much. Why?"

"What I'm about to tell you is for your ears only."

Millie's face lit with anticipation. "I'm listening."

Wendy leaned close, her voice barely above a whisper. The more she explained, the wider Millie's eyes grew. "What do you think?"

"Let me get this straight." Millie's eyes narrowed. "You want me to help you and Erica nudge Amanda into a romance without her ever finding out she's being nudged?"

"When you put it that way—"

"I assume you're aware that Amanda is smart enough to figure out what we're doing."

Wendy shrugged. "Which is why we have to be subtle."

"Do you and Erica have some sort of plan, or do you intend to fly by the seat of your pants?"

"We'll listen for opportunities to talk about the campaign and slip in Gary's name."

Millie raised a brow. "Is that what you call subtle?"

"Do you have a better idea?"

"Amanda expects me to hound her about dating, so I should take the lead."

Wendy aimed her palm at Millie. "Not so fast. This is a team effort, not a one-woman badgering campaign."

Millie scowled. "I don't badger."

"Yeah, you do."

"Then why are you including me?"

Time for a little ego massaging. Besides, she needed Millie to counter Erica's veto. "Because you know how to read subtle clues."

Millie's brows drew in. "Are you trying to butter me up?"

"Are you doubting our motivation?"

"Clever response." The hint of a grin appeared on Millie's face. "You're neither confirming nor denying."

"What do you expect from someone who's married to an attorney?" Wendy tapped her finger to her temple. "Besides, you've been around long enough to know there's a doggone good brain under all this blonde hair."

"Good point." Millie tapped her watch. "Our board meeting is scheduled to begin in ten minutes. Unless you want our partners to know about our secret snag-a-guy-for-Amanda meeting, I suggest you head next door. I'll follow a couple minutes later."

"Snag-a-guy-for-Amanda." Wendy's head tilted. "If you leave out the word for, it spells 'SAGA'."

"What is it with you and acronyms?"

"I'm just saying." Wendy slid off the stool. "I'll see you next door." She headed out the den's French doors to the back patio then on to the ranch house carport. After retrieving her laptop from her SUV, Wendy walked into the kitchen. "Hi."

Amanda filled her mug with coffee. "How's everything at the inn?"

Wendy froze. How did she know?

"I heard your car earlier."

Wendy blinked. Had Amanda noticed her reaction? "I wanted to make sure everything's ready for today's arrivals." She dropped Hilltop's key into the bowl.

Amanda stirred creamer and sugar into her coffee. "Did you talk to Millie?"

"Briefly." Hoping her tone hadn't given her away, Wendy ambled to the den and set her laptop on the table then sat beside Erica. "I have everything ready for today's meeting." Hopefully Awesam's CEO understood what she meant.

Erica shrugged. "You always show up prepared."

Wendy's brow pinched then released. Did she or didn't she understand?

Amanda ambled in and settled across from Wendy. "Millie plans to add a selection of appetizers to the private dining menu." She scooted her chair close to the table. "The bacon-wrapped dates she served to our Valentine couple were incredible."

Wendy opened her laptop. "Knowing Millie, she's already priced all of her suggestions."

Footsteps struck the kitchen floor, followed by Millie breezing in and setting a plate of cookies and her iPad on the table. "In addition to selecting and pricing four appetizers, I've created a list of wines we need to stock." She pulled out a chair between Wendy and Amanda. "Before we talk about business, I want to hear all about Amanda's new job as Keith Armstrong's campaign manager."

Wendy glared at Hilltop's chef. Was she seconds away from exposing SAGA?

Amanda shrugged. "There isn't much to tell. At least not yet."

Millie folded her arms on the table. "Keith will need a good team if he expects to win, especially when it comes to managing the money."

Erica shot Wendy what could only be interpreted as an 'I warned you about involving her' expression.

"You don't need to worry about the campaign, Millie." Amanda wrapped her fingers around her mug. "Keith recruited a bank president to function as his finance manager."

Millie's eyes remained trained on Amanda. "Someone I know?"

"Gary Redding."

"Aha." Millie snapped her fingers. "The good-looking bank president. Did you know he's divorced? There was quite a scandal when his wife up and left him."

Amanda glared at Millie. "I'm not interested in gossip, so enough talk about politics."

"Don't get all bent out of shape." Millie huffed. "I'm just saying he'd be a good catch."

"Not for me." Amanda opened her laptop. "We'll kick off today's meeting with Wendy's financial update."

So much for subtlety. Hoping Millie hadn't blown their plan, Wendy pulled up a spreadsheet and shared financial details. "Bottom line, we're under budget on expenses and over plan on profit."

"I have more good news." Erica tapped her keyboard. "Our occupancy rate continues to come in well above industry average."

"Not bad for a team of novices who didn't have a clue how to manage a business." Amanda leaned back. "Shows what smart women are capable of accomplishing, even against huge odds."

Wendy nodded. "If Gunter hadn't burned through all our money and mortgaged everything he owned, I would have spent this year's Valentine's Day alone in Gulfport wondering why my husband spent so much time away from home." She reached for a cookie. "Instead, I'm married to the most wonderful husband and father on the planet."

"And Erica is dating one of the most eligible guys in town," added Millie. "Moving here has done wonders for two out of three."

Amanda faced Millie, her jaw set. "If you're about to lecture me—"

"Hold on to your chickens, Madam President. I'm just saying Blue Ridge has been especially good for Erica and Wendy."

"Know what else would be especially good?" Erica's focus shifted from Millie to Amanda. "If we could have at least one staff meeting without you two bickering."

"I'm willing." Amanda faced Millie. "What about you?"

"Sure." Millie shrugged. "Why not?"

"All right, then." Erica leaned back. "Let's discuss a spring promotion." Ten minutes into the discussion the front door opened, followed by wheels rolling across the foyer and into the den. Abby offered a wave. "Tommy brought me home during my lunch break so I can join you."

Erica smiled at her daughter. "As Awesam's vice president, you always bring a fresh perspective to our meetings."

"The few times I've attended." Abby maneuvered onto a chair. "What did I interrupt?"

Erica pushed the wheelchair aside. "Plans for a spring promo."

Following another half-hour discussion and a unanimous vote, Abby grabbed a cookie and took a bite. "Scrumlicious as always."

Millie grinned. "If I'd known you were coming, I would have baked snickerdoodles."

"Chocolate chip are my second favorite. Although your cookies are only part of the reason I'm here, Millie." Abby set the half-eaten treat on the table. "I've been thinking a lot about that day I first saw my car after the accident—the way the side was caved in behind the passenger seat—I believed my life had been spared for a reason." Her eyes seemed to glaze over. "Then when I held Theo in my arms at the hospital—the way his tiny hand curled around my finger—I knew." She paused. "I understand this is a lot to ask of you all." Abby glanced around the table as if carefully considering her next words. "The reason I'm here...is because I want us to foster Theo."

Wendy exchanged a questioning look with Amanda.

Erica turned toward Abby. "Your heart's in the right place, sweetheart. However, taking care of an infant is a huge responsibility."

"Your mom's right." Amanda laced her fingers on the table. "Infants require constant care. Plus, I doubt we'd even qualify—"

"Are you kidding?" Wendy's focus shifted from Amanda to Erica. "We'd make great foster parents. Especially since there are four of us to help take care of a baby, five if Millie volunteers."

Millie nodded. "Think about Abby's proposal this way. You invited me and my kitties to stay with you after lightning caught my house on fire, so why not open your home to a helpless little baby? At least until some nice couple comes along to adopt him."

Erica reached for her daughter's hand. "This means a lot to you, doesn't it?"

"I've prayed a lot since we left Theo at the hospital, and now I believe in my heart he's one big reason I survived the accident."

"You're an amazing young woman." Erica's eyes remained focused on Abby. "Nothing's more important than caring for one of God's special children."

Wendy nodded. "As well as protecting him from an unpredictable, and sometimes cruel, foster system. For that reason I call for a vote to contact Child Services and tell them we've found the perfect home for Theo."

Millie's brows raised. "If I volunteer to help, will my vote count?"

Wendy snapped her fingers. "Absolutely."

"Then I vote yes."

Wendy nodded. "So do I. What about you, Erica?"

"Even though I'm a bit skeptical, I support my daughter."

"That's four yesses." Wendy turned toward Awesam's president. "This big a decision needs a unanimous vote."

"I know." Amanda released a long sigh. "Who am I to question divine guidance?"

"Amanda's vote makes five." Wendy reached across the table and tapped Abby's hand. "You have the go-ahead to contact Child Services."

"Actually—" Abby cleared her throat. "Earlier today I sort of talked to Allison, and well, her friend who works with Child Services is coming to interview us the day after tomorrow."

Amanda stared wide-eyed at Abby, then burst out laughing. "You were assuming we'd go along with your wild idea, weren't you?"

"To be honest, I knew Mom and Wendy would say yes."

"But you didn't know if I'd approve."

Millie scoffed. "Because our president is as stubborn as an old mule?"

Abby shook her head. "Because she's more logical than emotional."

"Seems our psychology student has learned a lot about human nature." A smile spread across Amanda's face as she reached for a cookie. "Besides, I prefer the term *tenacious*."

Millie rapped her fingers on the table. "If you weren't so tenacious, you'd give Gary Redding a second look."

Wendy's shoulders tightened. Why hadn't she listened to Erica?

"Tell you what, Millie." Amanda swallowed a bite of cookie. "If Mr. Redding shows one iota of interest…and that's one giant if…I'll consider accepting him as a male friend to stop your incessant badgering."

"All right then."

Wendy's shoulders relaxed. Maybe confiding in Awesam's chief information officer hadn't been a huge blunder after all.

Chapter 19

With Amanda, Wendy, and Millie in the back seat and Abby sitting beside her, Erica backed her daughter's car onto the street. At the stop sign, she turned toward Copperhill, Tennessee. "I spoke with Nancy yesterday. She'll interview the four of us about Hilltop, then conduct a separate interview with Abby."

"Is she aware that I'm an award-winning chef?"

Erica glanced at Millie in the rearview mirror. "I don't know."

"Doesn't matter if she does or doesn't," Amanda scoffed. "Our esteemed chef will find a way to slip the information into the conversation."

"Exactly." Millie snapped her fingers. "Because that's what a skillful interviewee does."

During the remainder of the drive, they reviewed their first Nancy's Nuggets interview and plans to promote Hilltop during their second. Twenty-five minutes after leaving home, Erica pulled onto the driveway beside a two-story frame house. She peered over her shoulder. "Are y'all ready?"

Millie nodded. "Today is my debut as an engaging podcast guest."

Amanda laughed. "Last year you didn't know beans about podcasts."

"Now I know all about this newfangled way to communicate." Millie lifted a small plastic food container off her lap and pushed her door open.

THE PROMISE

After Abby transferred to her wheelchair, Erica led the way to the front porch. Their slender, middle-aged interviewer swung the front door open before Erica had a chance to ring the bell. "My listeners are excited to hear all that's happened with you ladies since we last chatted." Nancy escorted them into a room off the foyer and seated everyone except Abby on one side of the table.

Millie placed the food container on the table then tapped the microphone in front of her chair. "Is this on?"

"Not yet." Nancy pointed to the mike on the other side of the table. "That one is for you, Abby. We'll talk one-on-one after I chat with your mom and the other ladies." After Abby maneuvered her chair in place, Nancy settled at the end of the table. "Remember to relax and treat this as a casual conversation among friends. When I address my questions to you by name, speak directly into the mike. Since this is your first time, Millie, do we need a quick practice round?"

She shook her head. "I listened to your podcast, so I know the drill."

"All right then. We have a couple of minutes until airtime. Any questions before we begin?"

"Yes." Millie scooted her chair close to the table. "How many people listen to your podcast?"

"On any given day, between one and two thousand."

"No kidding." Millie's eyes widened. "I had no idea you were that popular."

Nancy grinned. "Because I interview interesting people like you."

Millie's chest puffed.

Erica stifled a giggle.

"All right, ladies, I'm activating your microphones." After donning a headset and pressing a series of buttons, Nancy directed her guests to test their mikes. "We're all set. In five, four, three, two, one." She leaned close to her microphone. "Good afternoon, friends, and welcome to Nancy's Nuggets. Today we're fortunate to chat with three women you met on my podcast last year, along with two new guests. As you may recall, Amanda Smith, Erica Nelson, and Wendy Thomason—now Wendy Armstrong—met for the first time during the once-in-a century blizzard that blanketed North Georgia. During those few days they learned a man known as Gunter had deceived them. When they returned home they each discovered their homes had been foreclosed. Refusing to become victims, these brave ladies returned to Blue Ridge, created the Awesam company, and transformed a home in poor repair into the Hilltop Inn. Amanda, what most excites you about managing a luxurious bed and breakfast?"

"Other than celebrating everything we've accomplished during the past year, meeting so many wonderful guests excites me the most."

"What is one of the most memorable moments you've experienced as an innkeeper, Erica?"

Should she mention a short version of the broken engagement incident? Why not? "After one of our guests checked in with her fiancé and came to terms with him being an abusive man, we helped her summon the courage to break off the engagement and send him packing."

"Saving a woman from future injuries must have been satisfying."

Erica nodded. "For all of us." *Especially given the man was the ex she and Abby had escaped from years earlier.*

"Since our last conversation, Wendy, you married the attorney you first met during the blizzard and gave birth to a son. Tell us about your experiences."

Wendy's face lit with a smile. "Chris and I were married in Hilltop Inn's gazebo with our family and close friends in attendance. A few weeks later after Ryan was born, Chris adopted him as his son."

"What a wonderful gift for a newborn."

"Chris is an amazing father. Amanda is Ryan's adoptive grandmother, Erica is his aunt, and her daughter Abby is his cousin."

"You ladies have reinvented the meaning of family."

"By the way, the gazebo where Chris and I exchanged vows is the perfect venue for an intimate wedding in an English country garden followed by a reception catered by our award-winning chef."

Millie leaned close to the microphone. "That's me. I'm also Ryan's honorary great grandmother."

Nancy smiled. "How did you become involved with these ladies?"

"I live next door to Hilltop Inn, which was originally a vacation home owned by my best friend Eleanor Harrington and her husband. God rest their souls. Anyway, when I learned that three strangers planned to turn the house into a commercial property, I threatened to boycott their rezoning effort. Lucky for me and for them, they discovered my talent as a cook and offered me a job as the inn's chef."

"I assume you abandoned the boycott."

Millie eyed Nancy as if she had asked a ridiculous question. "Of course. Now I'm on Awesam's board as chief information officer."

"Wendy referred to you as an award-winning chef—"

"My chocolate peppermint cake won the first annual Hilltop Inn Dessert Competition. This November I'll serve as the head judge." Millie peeled the lid off the food container, releasing vanilla and cinnamon aromas. "These are my snickerdoodle cookies, Abby's favorite." She pushed the container to Nancy. "Try one."

"All right." Nancy took a bite. "Oh my goodness, this is delicious." Following another twenty minutes of questions and answers about the inn, she signaled a thumbs-up. "Thank you for bringing my listeners up-to-date on your adventures, ladies. Following a brief commercial break, I'll chat with Erica's daughter, Abby, and learn about two miracles that have impacted her young life." After deactivating the mikes, she faced Abby. "Are you ready to share your stories?"

"Yes, ma'am."

"Excellent." A minute passed. Nancy pressed two buttons then counted down from three. "I'm delighted to introduce an amazing young woman who survived a serious accident late last year. Abby, what can you tell us about the day your car was totaled?"

Abby leaned close to the mike and top lined the accident.

Emotion gripped Erica as her child shared details about her physical therapy and adapting to life in a wheelchair.

Abby paused for a brief moment. "I've made a lot of progress, which is why I'm confident I will one day walk again."

"You're a determined young woman. Tell us about the second miracle in your life."

A serene smile spread across her face. "His name is Theo. Mom and I found him on the steps outside the building where I work." Abby relayed details about his birth defect as well as her and Erica's experience in the hospital.

"You were clearly meant to find this child."

Abby nodded. "Theo is one reason God spared my life. Is it okay if I tell everyone about the GoFundMe page to raise money for Theo's surgery?"

"Absolutely."

Following an emotional appeal, Abby paused for a brief moment. "If Theo's mother is listening, we want you to know that your beautiful baby will be loved and cared for by a family who understands how special he is."

Nancy dabbed at her eyes. "A miracle infant rescued by an amazing mother-and-daughter team. Thank you for sharing your story, Abby. To everyone who tuned in today, please donate whatever you are able to this worthy cause. Be sure to tune in tomorrow to hear about a local charity that rescues stray animals. Until then stay safe and take time to hug your loved ones." Nancy deactivated the microphones and removed her headset. "Thank you for another stimulating conversation, ladies. Abby and Erica, will you come back in a few months and give my audience an update on Theo?"

Erica's eyes met her daughter's. Abby signaled a thumbs-up. Erica drew in a deep satisfying breath, then turned toward Nancy. "You can count on us."

"Excellent." Nancy escorted her guests to the door.

Halfway back to Abby's car, Millie snapped her fingers. "I have a great idea."

Amanda grinned. "You're planning to start your own podcast?"

Millie huffed. "Maybe one day I will. But today, since Bernie's covering for us at Hilltop, why don't we play tourist and roam around Copperhill and McCaysville for a couple of hours."

Wendy shrugged. "Linda has Ryan for the afternoon, so I'm free."

"So am I," added Abby.

"All right then, let's go."

As Millie closed the distance to Abby's car, Amanda linked arms with Erica. "By the time we head back to Blue Ridge, Millie will make sure everyone in these two towns knows she's an award-winning chef at the fabulous Hilltop Inn."

Erica chuckled. "Our one-woman publicity committee." *And not-so-secret matchmaker.*

Chapter 20

Thirty minutes before the Child Services representative was scheduled to arrive, the ranch household buzzed with activity. Erica vacuumed the last room then stashed the vacuum cleaner in the hall closet. Wendy continued dusting while Amanda finished cleaning the kitchen.

The decadent aroma of chocolate floated around Millie as she dashed in from the carport and carried a plate of freshly baked brownies to the dining room table. "My contribution to our strategy."

Amanda followed Millie into the den. "Those smell delicious and create a homey atmosphere. However, we need to rely on our credibility, not gimmicks, to convince Child Services we're fit to foster."

"Yeah, well." Millie propped a hand on her hip. "Sweet bribes are akin to adding whipped cream atop a big ole slice of pumpkin pie."

Amanda mirrored Millie's stance. "That is one whacky analogy."

Millie huffed. "Not for an award-winning chef."

"Maybe you should start your own podcast and call it the Millie Cunningham self-promotion hour."

"You'd be my first guest. Amanda Smith, the forty-four-year-old woman who's too stubborn to look for a man."

Erica moved between them. "Either you two play nice with each other or go to your rooms."

Amanda laughed. "We're just having a little fun, right, Chef Millie?"

"Absolutely."

Abby wheeled into the den. "What's going on?"

Millie lowered her arms to her sides. "Your mother is scolding two naughty board members."

Abby's eyes widened. "Because you and Amanda were arguing?"

"Teasing, not arguing."

"Okay, then." Abby maneuvered her body onto the sofa. "We have enough going on without my wheelchair adding to the distraction."

"I'll take care of it, sweetheart. "Erica pushed the chair to her daughter's room. Doubt crept in as she peered around the space. The beanbag chair had been Abby's favorite reading spot before the accident. The teddy bear with a pink ribbon tied around its neck was propped on her bed—the only toy her child had taken with her when they sought refuge in a Baltimore women's shelter all those years ago. How would Abby react if Child Services found them unsuitable to foster an infant?

The doorbell rang. Erica's heart pounded in her chest as she scrambled to the foyer and pulled the door open. A dark-haired young woman clutched a clipboard to her chest. "I'm Ms. Abernathy, Child Services caseworker, and you are?"

"Erica Nelson." She extended her hand.

The woman's grip was firm. "You're one of the women who rescued the abandoned infant."

"Yes, along with my daughter. Welcome to our home."

"Thank you." Ms. Abernathy released her hand then stepped into the foyer and peered into the living room functioning as Awesam's office.

"We've been looking forward to meeting you." Erica led the caseworker to the den. After introducing the rest of the team, she motioned to a club chair. "Please have a seat."

"Thank you." The woman charged with judging them settled across from Wendy and glanced around the room. "Dr. Allison Baker speaks highly of you all."

Wendy smiled. "Allison is my sister-in-law—"

"Yes, I know. She's also the reason I'm responding to your petition."

Erica settled between Abby and Amanda. How much did this woman already know about them?

The caseworker laid her clipboard on her lap. "I have a number of questions, beginning with why you ladies want to take on the challenging task of fostering a newborn."

"I'd like to respond first." Grateful they had anticipated that question, Erica leaned forward and met the caseworker's eyes. "Even though we aren't what most people would call typical, we are a closeknit family. Plus, during the past thirteen months we have each faced and overcome difficult challenges."

Ms. Abernathy nodded. "I know your stories."

Amanda raised a brow. "Then you know we're survivors, Ms. Abernathy. Who better to care for an abandoned child?"

As would be expected of a professional, the caseworker clicked a pen then proceeded to make a note on the document attached to her clipboard.

Wendy scooted to the edge of her chair. "Are you aware that I was raised in foster homes?"

"I am."

"Then you also know that I understand what children relegated to the system need to thrive. Another fact in our favor, four of us are mothers who have experience taking care of babies."

Ms. Abernathy scribed another note. "How do you fit into this picture, Ms. Cunningham?"

"I'm Grammy Millie, the honorary great grandmother in this nontraditional family." She aimed her thumb toward the hall. "I lived in the guest room for months while my fire-damaged home underwent repairs. So I can testify to their good characters."

"I see." Ms. Abernathy made a note on her clipboard. "I've heard from everyone except you, Abby. Given your job, your studies, and your physical therapy schedule, why do you want to assume more responsibility?"

Erica stared at the woman. Was there anything she didn't know about their lives?

Abby tilted her head. "Do you believe in divine intervention, Ms. Abernathy?"

She seemed to peer into Abby's eyes. "I do."

"Then you understand why Theo's mother left him on the crisis center doorstep. After Mom and I spent hours comforting him in the hospital, I understood that finding him was only the beginning of my responsibility."

"Speaking of the hospital—" Ms. Abernathy pulled her phone from her pocket and tapped the screen. "Every day since Theo was admitted, this woman has shown up outside the viewing room." She handed the phone to Wendy. "Do you recognize her?"

Wendy shook her head then carried the phone to Abby.

"Neither do I." Abby passed the phone to her mother.

Erica studied the young girl's thin shoulders and pained expression. "Is it possible she's Theo's mother?"

"Possibly. Although she hasn't spoken to anyone." Ms. Abernathy tapped her clipboard. Following a dozen more questions and answers, she paused for a long moment. "If we were to grant your request, which one of you would be the child's primary caretaker?"

Millie snapped her fingers. "Some folks claim it takes a village to raise a child. The five of us are Theo's village."

Abby leaned forward on her elbows. "Millie's right." The golden retriever padded over and sprawled at her feet. Abby reached down and stroked her pet's back. "In case you're worried about my dog, Dusty is as gentle as a kitten around Wendy's baby."

"Good to know." Their caseworker stood. "I'd like to see more of your home."

"I'll give you the tour." Erica led her to the kitchen then to Awesam's office. "We manage our business from home, so one of us is always present."

"I see."

They moved on to the guest room. Wendy had placed Ryan's cradle beside the bed and a new baby monitor on the nightstand. "Abby, Amanda, and I will share the daily responsibilities for Theo."

Ms. Abernathy ambled to the dresser and fingered the pad converting the furniture to a changing table. "Given your daughter's medical situation, how will she be able to care for an infant?"

Erica's back stiffened. "Other than driving, Abby is completely self-sufficient." Hoping her tone hadn't come across as judgmental, she tapped a pad Wendy had placed on the bed. "As you can see, we've created a second changing area accessible to a wheelchair. Who better to help care for an abandoned infant than a young woman who has overcome a tragic accident?"

"I understand why you want to support your daughter; however, I can't help but wonder—" Ms. Abernathy spun away from the dresser. "Would you and the other women have petitioned to foster if Abby hadn't insisted?"

Erica broke eye contact. "Wendy was alone and pregnant when the four of us moved into this house. We were ready to help care for her child." She rocked the cradle the Awesam family had given to Wendy. "Now we have the same opportunity with Theo."

"That's an explanation, not an answer."

Erica forced her thoughts into submission. "I don't mean to offend, but the question is irrelevant."

"How so?"

"Theo needs a loving family to care for him. At least temporarily." Erica caught their caseworker's eye. "I believe beyond the shadow of a doubt that we are that family."

Ms. Abernathy remained silent for a long moment, then tucked her clipboard under her arm and returned to the den. "I appreciate your time, ladies. I'll have a decision by the end of the week."

"Before you leave, I have something for you." Millie rushed to the kitchen, then returned to the den. She'd packed all the brownies in a plastic container. Now she handed the bribe to Ms. Abernathy. "One of my specialties."

"Thank you." The woman charged with judging if they were qualified to foster Theo smiled for the first time since she had entered their home.

Erica escorted their guest to the front door. "Please let us know if you have additional questions."

"Thank you. However, I have all the information I need."

After closing the door, Erica returned to the den and hiked her hip on the sofa arm beside Abby. "We've done all we can."

Millie nodded. "In my opinion as Awesam's chief information officer, my brownies guarantee we're a shoo-in."

"Only if Ms. Abernathy has a sweet tooth." Amanda stood and stretched. "It's time to head next door and wait to welcome today's arriving guests."

"I'll walk out with you." Millie grabbed her coat off the back of a dining room chair then looped her hand around Amanda's elbow. "You know, a bank president is a good catch—"

"Ugh." Amanda yanked her arm from Millie's grip then rushed through the kitchen and out the back door.

Wendy bolted from her chair. "Millie!"

Hilltop Inn's chef spun around. "What?"

"We need to talk."

Abby peered over her shoulder as Wendy steered Hilltop's chef into the kitchen. "Wendy clued Millie in on Linda's plan, didn't she?"

Erica sighed. "Against my better judgement."

Moments after the back door slammed shut, Wendy returned to the den. "I should have listened to you."

Resisting the urge to agree, Erica rose. "Chances are Millie would hound Amanda, even if we hadn't brought her into the loop."

"I suppose you're right. Anyway, I need to relieve my mother-in-law of babysitting duty." Wendy lifted her purse off the coffee table and headed toward the front door. "Keep me posted on Child Services' decision."

"We will." Abby peered up at Erica. "Will you bring me my ride, Mom? I'm taking the rest of the afternoon off to catch up on my studies."

"Of course." After retrieving the wheelchair and waiting for her daughter to roll to her room, Erica headed to Awesam's office. She settled at the desk and opened her laptop. The black ring box hidden in her dresser drawer played in her mind as she pulled up her private spreadsheet. Her fingers hovered over the keyboard. If Ms. Abernathy found in their favor, her life was days away from another monumental shift. Before she could change her mind, she added a second reason why accepting Brad's proposal would have to wait.

By the time Wendy turned onto the Armstrongs' driveway, her frustration with Millie had vanished. After all, the snag-a-guy-for-Amanda ploy had been her mother-in-law's idea, not hers. Should she tell Linda about her idea to support SAGA? Best to keep that bit of information secret. At least for a while. Wendy pocketed her key. She reached for her purse the moment her phone rang. The tone wasn't on her favorites list. Should she ignore it or find out who was calling? Curiosity won out. She pulled the phone from her purse. Her brow pinched. Why was her father's wife calling?

Wendy swiped her finger across the screen and pressed FaceTime. "Hey, Donna."

"Douglas knows about me visiting you."

Wendy's shoulders tensed. Was her stepmother merely informing her or warning her? "How did he find out?"

"He saw the Hilltop Inn charge on my credit card bill." Donna sighed. "Maybe subconsciously I wanted him to know."

And me to know he knew? Wendy pictured Douglas Hewitt facing his wife with his arms folded across his chest. "How did he react?"

"With a stern warning not to mention your existence to our boys or to anyone else in his family—to protect his reputation." Donna scoffed. "Rich considering all the years of his infidelity."

Pain erupted in the back of Wendy's throat. If she hadn't asked her mother-in-law to help find her father—but she had, and now she had to live with rejection from both of her parents. "Did he forbid you from talking to me?"

"He tried until I told him you and Ryan are part of *my* family." Donna paused. "My boys deserve to know they have a sister and a cousin."

"Are you planning to tell them about me?"

"When the time is right. In the meantime, my husband has no say about my relationship with you or my grandson."

Donna's heartfelt tone brought a smile to Wendy's face. "I'm glad."

"So am I. Is there anything new and exciting going on in your life?"

"Actually, there is." Wendy shared details about Theo. "Every once in a while, I wonder how different my life would be if my mother had given me up as an infant." She peered in the rearview mirror at her little guy's car seat. "Until I realize how blessed I am to have so many wonderful people in my life. Including you."

"We were meant to find each other. My boys just came home from school." Donna's voice lowered. "We'll talk more later." She ended the call.

After tossing her phone on the passenger seat, Wendy made her way to the Armstrongs' porch and rang the doorbell.

Linda responded, carrying her grandson in her arms. "How'd the interview go?"

"As well as could be expected, I suppose. How's my little guy?"

"As adorable as always." She placed Ryan in Wendy's arms. He yawned. "Seem's he's ready for an afternoon nap."

"Thank you for taking care of him for me."

"I loved every minute."

After slipping a jacket on her child, Wendy carried him to the car and secured him in his car seat. "I want you to know that your mommy and daddy will always be here for you."

A sweet smile lit her little guy's face. "Mama."

"Oh my gosh." Happy tears pooled as Wendy pressed her hand to her heart. "That's the first time you've called me mama." She kissed her child's cheek. "I love you more than words can possibly express."

Chapter 21

The call came in three days after the interview while Erica was alone at the ranch house. Her palms turned clammy as she stared at her ringing phone. Should she answer or let the call go to voicemail? If she didn't answer and the news wasn't favorable, she'd have time to think. On the other hand, if she answered, she could ask questions. Erica breathed deeply then swiped her hand across the screen and pressed the phone to her ear. "Hello, Ms. Abernathy."

"Hi, Erica."

Was the woman's less formal version of hello a good sign? Erica meandered to the sliding glass doors overlooking the backyard. Dusty sprawled on the patio soaking in the sun. "Do you need more information, or do you have additional questions?"

"Thank you for asking, but no. As I explained during our initial meeting, you and your partners aren't the type of family we usually approve for fostering." The Child Services caseworker paused.

What did she mean by usually approve? Erica wiped a sweaty palm on her jeans. Why hadn't she let the call go to voicemail?

"Our ultimate goal is for a traditional family to step up and go through the adoption process. Of course there's always the possibility that one or both of the child's parents will have a change of heart. Given the way

Theo was left on a doorstep, either would present a whole different set of challenges." Another uncomfortable pause.

Erica shifted her weight from one leg to the other. Was the woman who held Theo's fate in her hands trying to soften the blow of rejection?

"Until and unless either of those events occur, Theo needs a home. After reviewing my notes and taking Allison Baker's recommendation into account, we believe your nontraditional family is well qualified to foster the child."

Erica blinked. Had she heard correctly? "Are you saying we're approved?"

"Are you questioning our decision?"

Why had she questioned it? "I just wanted to make sure I understood."

"To clarify what I said, yes, you and your partners are now foster parents."

Relief washed over Erica. "Thank you for trusting us."

"Your daughter's comment about divine intervention also helped tip the scales in your favor. As to the schedule, a nurse will bring Theo to your home tomorrow at noon. She'll show you the proper way to feed an infant with a cleft lip. In a few minutes, I'll email you a list of items one of you ladies needs to purchase before then."

Erica turned her back toward the sliding glass door. "I'll take care of everything."

"Excellent. I'll contact you next week to schedule my first follow-up visit. In the meantime, you're welcome to call me if a problem arises."

Moments after the call ended, Erica texted her partners. "We're approved. Theo arriving tomorrow at noon."

Abby responded with a heart emoji. Amanda with a thumbs up. Millie's message reflected her standard reaction to both good and bad news. Desserts. "I'll bake brownies to celebrate." Erica pocketed her phone.

Their chef had no idea that most of her baked goodies ended up at the crisis center.

A sudden sense of urgency sent Erica scrambling to Awesam's office. Amanda and Abby had agreed she was best suited to create a detailed take-care-of-Theo schedule. Thankfully, Wendy had made a list of tasks newborns required. Now she had to put everything together. Erica tapped her laptop keypad and opened a blank Excel spreadsheet. After completing the first month's assignments, she printed four copies then moved the cradle into her room. Hopefully her partners would appreciate her assuming responsibility for the infant's first two nights in their home.

Conflicting emotions rattled Amanda as she pocketed her phone and dropped onto one of Hilltop Inn's front porch rocking chairs. Babysitting Ryan for a few hours at a time was a far cry from caring for an infant twenty-four-seven. Especially given how much she valued her independence. At least she and her partners would share the responsibility. Amanda's focus shifted to the elderly couple holding hands as they headed up the sidewalk. She stood to greet them as they climbed onto the porch. "How's your second day visiting our town going?"

The woman patted her tummy. "The Blue Ridge Mountain food tour was fabulous. We especially enjoyed talking with chefs and restaurant owners."

Her husband grinned. "Now we need a nap before heading back to town for dessert."

Amanda unlocked the door and held it open. How many naps would caring for an infant require? "Enjoy the rest of your afternoon."

Watching the gentleman escort his wife up the stairs tugged on Amanda's heartstrings. The day she married Preston, she had imagined them growing old together. Strolling hand in hand on the path running beside the Mississippi river. Dining at their favorite restaurants. Now all she had were memories.

Enough with the melancholy. Amanda drew in a deep breath as she returned to the front porch rocking chair. A black cat sprang onto the railing. "Are you the mysterious kitty some of our guests have asked about?" The feline meowed. "I'll take that as a yes." Amanda set her chair in motion. Innkeeping, managing a political campaign, helping care for an abandoned child, and talking to stray cats filled her life now.

A white sedan turned onto the driveway and eased past the corner of the inn. Moments later, Amanda met the first of two new arrivals at the top of the steps. "Welcome to Hilltop Inn."

The older of the two women climbed onto the porch. "My daughter and I have been looking forward to this trip for months."

The woman who appeared to be in her twenties hauled her suitcase up the stairs. "My mother believes a shopping spree in a quaint town far away from home is the perfect way for me to recover from my divorce."

"We're delighted you've chosen to stay with us." Amanda unlocked the front door and led them to the check-in desk. "We'll do our best to make your stay memorable." After sharing details about the inn and escorting the guests to the Bluebell Suite, Amanda returned to the porch. The black cat sprang off the railing and rubbed against her leg. "If you're looking for someone to adopt you, you need to cozy up to our cat-loving chef, not me." The feline meowed, then curled up on the top step.

Amanda settled on the rocking chair. She pulled her phone from her pocket and texted her daughter. "We're approved to foster Theo."

Ten minutes later Morgan texted back. "Congratulations. Kevin and I plan to drive to Blue Ridge Saturday morning and stay until Sunday afternoon."

She hadn't seen her daughter and son-in-law since Christmas. "I'll have the guest room ready for you." Amanda punctuated the text message with a smiley face then set her chair in motion to wait for the next arrivals.

After responding to her mom's text, Abby slid her phone back into her jeans pocket.

Anna, her physical therapist, who had become a close friend and confidante caught Abby's eye. "Good news?"

Abby nodded. "We were approved to foster Theo."

"Wow. Congratulations!"

Abby understood the sacrifice everyone was making to fulfill her wish. "There's no way I could take on the responsibility without my family's help."

"Their commitment, as well as yours, is admirable." Anna resumed the rehabilitation regime everyone hoped would eventually heal Abby's spinal cord injury. "How's the GoFundMe campaign going?"

"We have a couple of grand so far."

"Good beginning."

Abby flinched at a sudden stab of pain.

Anna's brows raised. "You felt that, didn't you?"

"Big time. Is that a good sign?"

"The best possible."

Her therapist's expression helped reignite the hope that had begun to wane after Abby and Tommy ushered in the new year.

"How do you suppose Tommy will respond to the news about Theo?"

"Like a champ." Despite his unwavering loyalty, deep down Abby believed Tommy deserved to spend his life with a woman who could walk and dance and drive her own car. Even though it would smash her heart into a thousand pieces, if she was still bound to a wheelchair by next New Years Eve, she vowed to end their relationship.

"Speaking of champs." Anna nodded toward the entrance.

"How's everything going?"

Abby's pulse accelerated as she turned toward the sound of Tommy's voice. "My therapist hit a nerve."

"Literally." Anna grinned. "Which means her spinal cord is continuing to heal."

A smile lit Tommy's face. "I'm guessing before the end of the year we'll be back on the hiking trails. Any update on Theo?"

Abby nodded. "We'll become a foster family at noon tomorrow."

Tommy reached for her hand. "Next summer we'll take him on a train ride."

Fearing tears were on the verge of erupting, Abby looked away. "How's work going?"

"Nothing new."

Anna lifted Abby's foot. "Time for your toe maneuver."

Abby closed her eyes and concentrated on moving her big toe while secretly praying for a miracle before she had to break her and Tommy's hearts.

Chapter 22

Six hours after Theo's midnight feeding, his cry nudged Amanda's eyes open. Yawning, she peeled back her blanket and swung her legs over the side of the bed. "This is why women my age don't have babies. At least not on purpose," she mumbled under her breath as she turned on the bedside lamp. Amanda lifted the infant from his cradle and tiptoed down the hall toward the aroma of freshly brewed coffee and light spilling from the empty den. After preparing Theo's bottle, Amanda settled on the sofa. Pleased she had at least mastered the technique of bottle feeding a cleft-lip baby, she propped her sock-clad feet on the coffee table. "Time for breakfast, Little Pip."

Erica padded down the hall and headed straight to the kitchen without uttering a word. After meandering to the den, settling on a club chair, and sipping her coffee, she found her voice. "How did your first baby-duty night go?"

"As expected. You're up early."

"We have an inn full of guests next door and today is Bernie's day off, so I need to help serve breakfast. Then I have late morning and early afternoon massage clients. When are Morgan and Kevin due to arrive?"

"Sometime before lunch, depending on the traffic leaving Atlanta. Millie volunteered to cook dinner tonight. You're welcome to join us."

"Thanks for the invitation, but I have a date with Brad."

"Are you any closer to opening the ring box?"

"Not with Theo in the picture." Erica sipped her coffee.

"Our Little Pip has no idea he's thwarting a romance."

Erica's brow pinched. "Who's Pip?"

"The orphan from *Great Expectations*. I read the story in high school."

"So did I. Anyway, our little orphan is delaying not thwarting my relationship with Brad."

"Either way, he's a disruption." Amanda lifted Theo to her shoulder and patted his back.

"Speaking of disruption, what's happening with the campaign?"

"Not much until the word's out. We have another planning meeting scheduled for next week. If Keith is elected, at some point he and Chris will end up on opposite sides of a case."

"Who do you suppose would win that legal battle?"

Amanda shrugged. "Depends on whether the defendant is innocent or guilty, or which attorney presents the best closing argument."

"I wouldn't want to sit on that jury."

"That makes two of us."

"Enough talk about politics. I need to prepare for today's innkeeping duties." Erica lifted off the club chair and headed toward the hall.

"I'm right behind you." After carrying Theo to her room and changing his diaper, Amanda swaddled and laid him down. "At least I'll have time to shower and dress before your morning snack." She rocked the cradle until his eyes closed. "Sleep tight, Little Pip." Amanda switched on the monitor then walked out, leaving the door ajar.

She headed straight to the bathroom and turned on the shower spigot. The moment steam escaped around the glass enclosure, she stepped into the tub. As the hot water cascaded down her body, her mind drifted to the last anniversary she had celebrated with her soulmate. Enjoying two deliciously romantic nights at a New Orleans bed and breakfast while Morgan stayed with a friend. Despite the hot water, a shiver raced through her limbs as the memory morphed to her wedding night with the man she believed was Paul Sullivan. Until she met Erica and Wendy and discovered his true identity. She had gambled on a second marriage and lost. No way she'd risk another romantic relationship.

After showering and dressing, Amanda carried the book she'd begun reading to the den and settled on the club chair until Theo's whimpers called her back to baby duty.

Halfway between eleven and twelve, the back door opened followed by footsteps striking the kitchen floor. "We're here."

Amanda laid Theo on the sofa and rushed to embrace Morgan then Kevin. "You both look wonderful."

"So do you, Mom."

Dusty scampered from the hall ahead of Abby.

Morgan patted Dusty's head then bent down to hug her honorary sister. "I can't wait to catch up on everything going on with you."

"We'll talk tomorrow morning. Tommy's on his way over to pick me up. We're spending the day with a couple of our high school friends who are home from college for the weekend." Abby nodded toward her dog padding to the den then sitting between the sofa and the coffee table. "Dusty has assumed the role as our newest family member's protector."

"I'm ready to meet him." Morgan stepped over Dusty, then settled on the sofa and lifted the infant into her arms.

Amanda leaned over her daughter's shoulder. "Little Pip, meet my daughter."

Morgan laughed. "You nicknamed him after a fictional character?"

"Who's also an orphan. Besides, Little Guy belongs to Ryan."

"Well, whatever you call him, he's adorable."

"Other than his birth defect, he's perfect." Abby maneuvered her wheelchair beside the sofa. "Touch his palm, and he'll melt your heart."

"Oh my gosh." A smile lit Morgan's face as Theo's tiny hand curled around her finger. "I can't imagine what was going on in his mother's head when she dumped him at the crisis center."

Amanda straightened. "At least she had enough love in her heart to leave him where she knew he'd be found."

Kevin sat beside Morgan and peered at Abby. "Any news about his surgery?"

"Tuesday, Mom and I have an appointment with a local plastic surgeon."

"Hopefully by then, we'll have raised enough money to cover the cost." Amanda skirted the sofa and settled on a club chair.

Millie breezed in through the back door. "Welcome back to Blue Ridge."

Morgan peered over her shoulder. "Hey, Millie."

"I brought you and Abby your favorite lunch."

Kevin grinned. "Let me guess, mac and cheese."

"With a little added surprise." Millie set the baking dish on the counter and turned on the oven before ambling to the den. "After lunch I'll take care of Theo to give you and your mom plenty of time to visit."

"Thank you, Millie. You're a sweetheart."

"Yeah, I know. How much has your mother told you about her job as Keith Armstrong's campaign manager?"

"Kevin and I have been so busy with work and our new house, Mom and I haven't had much time to talk."

Millie hiked her hip on the sofa arm. "Lucky for her, she's partnering with a local bank president, who's also a good looking, middle-aged, divorced gentleman."

Amanda scoffed. "Our not-so-subtle chief information officer has this ridiculous idea about some sort of romance developing between Gary and me."

Millie propped a hand on her hip. "If you weren't so all-fired determined to remain single, you might enjoy a little hanky-panky."

Morgan peered up at Millie. "Is that how your generation described fooling around?"

"I'm just saying your mother would be wise to keep her options open."

Morgan's focus shifted from Millie to Amanda then back to Millie. "I know you mean well, and I don't mean any disrespect. However, Mom is an accomplished, intelligent woman who knows what's best for her. So giving her unsolicited advice about her personal life is a total waste of time."

Amanda pressed her palms together. "Thank you for enlightening our overzealous chef, honey."

"Except—" Millie pursed her lips as if debating how to finish her sentence.

Amanda's shoulders tensed. "Except what?" Her tone challenged.

Millie eyed Amanda. "It's time to cook the mac and cheese."

"What's the extra ingredient?" asked Kevin.

"Hickory-smoked bacon." Millie lifted off the sofa arm and hustled to the kitchen.

"Save some for me." Responding to the doorbell, Abby wheeled toward the foyer. Moments later, she returned with Tommy by her side. After the two young couples spent a half-hour catching up, Abby and her boyfriend headed out the front door.

"Despite all the commotion, Little Pip has fallen asleep."

"At least until he's hungry again." After carrying Theo to his room and tucking him into his cradle, Amanda returned to the den and sat beside Morgan. "I want to hear all about your new house."

Morgan's face beamed. "It's a two-story brick with a basement on a cul-de-sac in a quiet neighborhood." Morgan and Kevin's enthusiasm as they described their home conjured memories of Amanda's life with Preston. Except her daughter's first home was far grander than the two-bedroom shotgun house she and the love of her life had renovated.

During lunch and again while enjoying dinner, Millie refrained from uttering a word about Amanda's love life or anyone related to the campaign—giving Amanda hope Morgan's comment had ended Millie's meddling.

Chapter 23

Nine days after she and her partners assumed roles as foster parents, Erica donned jeans, a sweater, and tennis shoes then turned off her bedroom light and headed to the den.

Millie looked up from feeding Theo. "Brad's obviously not taking you to a fancy restaurant tonight."

Erica propped her hip on the sofa arm. "A fundraising cookout at the high school followed by the varsity basketball game."

"Not exactly what I'd call a romantic date. Although as the principal, I suppose he's obligated to be there."

"Brad's son and Ashley are joining us."

"Are they officially a couple now?"

"Jimmy moved into her apartment, so what do you think?"

"They should get married. That's what I think."

Amanda strode through the kitchen from the carport. "The late arrivals are settled in. Thanks for helping with Theo, Millie."

Millie glanced over her shoulder. "Feeding and rocking Little Pip is easy. Changing his diaper is another story."

Erica lifted off the sofa arm. "Maybe Abby's podcast interview will attract a traditional family who wants to adopt him."

"We can hope." Amanda settled at the dining room table and tapped her laptop keyboard. "Our GoFundMe campaign is generating a lot of interest."

Erica eased behind Amanda and peered at the screen. "A few more weeks and we should have enough money to cover the surgery." Responding to the doorbell, Erica headed to the foyer. "I'll see y'all later." She opened the door and tapped the varsity letter on Brad's jacket. "From your days as a winning football coach or star player?"

"The former." Brad pressed his hand to her back and nodded toward his sixteen-year-old SUV as they headed toward the driveway. "I hope you don't mind Jimmy and Ashley riding with us."

"A double date sounds like fun."

He opened the passenger door. "This vehicle isn't as exciting as the Corvette, but a lot easier to climb into."

"True." Erica climbed onto the seat and turned toward the younger version of his father sitting beside the stunning brunette she had first laid eyes on at Jimmy's trial. "It's nice to see you both again."

"It's been a while."

Ashley stole a quick glance at Jimmy. "We're both wondering how Abby's therapy is going."

Determined to paint the rosiest picture possible, Erica forced a smile. "She's making excellent progress. I assume you've heard about the abandoned infant."

Jimmy nodded. "By now, at least half the town knows about Theo."

Brad slid behind the steering wheel. "News travels fast." He backed down the driveway. During the drive, the guys talked about basketball and the high school's chances to make the regional playoffs.

Erica's shoulders tensed the moment they pulled into the already full parking lot. Memories of the last time she had stepped foot inside the school raced through her head. Walking into Brad's office after seeing Abby's totaled car for the first time. Explaining how they needed to discover if their relationship was strong enough to survive their children's accident. Erica peered at Brad's profile. Hearing him refer to her as 'my love' for the first time. She turned away. How long would he wait for her to accept his proposal?

Brad pulled into his reserved parking space. "One of the perks of being the principal." He and Jimmy climbed out, circled the SUV, and opened the passenger doors.

Ashley slid off her seat. "Your parents raised a gentleman."

Jimmy shrugged. "Southern values."

Ashley clung to Jimmy's arm while they headed to the school's main entrance. Erica and Brad walked behind the young couple. Why didn't Brad hold her hand? Did Jimmy's cane serve as too stark a reminder of the accident that had seriously injured his son and her daughter? Or did he consider a show of affection inappropriate in his workplace?

Inside, Brad greeted folks by name as they made their way toward a multitude of voices spilling into the hallway. A man and a woman sat at a table beside the cafeteria entrance collecting money. "Erica Nelson, meet Ms. Emerson, one of our parents, and Mr. Wagner, a faculty member. They're cochairs for this fundraiser."

The attractive thirty-something woman's eyes sparkled as she smiled at Brad, then eyed Erica. "You're Abby's mother, aren't you?"

Erica's brow pinched then released. "I am."

"I'm Bridget. Our daughters are friends. Abby is such a delightful young woman. I hear she's studying child psychology."

Had Brad told her, or had her daughter's educational pursuit become public knowledge after the accident? "She is."

"Given her personality, she's chosen the perfect career." Ms. Emerson turned toward Brad's son. "Who's your lovely lady friend?"

"Ashley Bowman."

"Ah, yes. From your trial."

Erica struggled to avoid staring at the woman. At least her comment answered one question.

"Ms. Bowman will join our faculty in a few weeks," added Brad.

Mr. Wagner extended his hand to Ashley. "Welcome aboard."

"Thank you. I'm looking forward to working with the staff."

Bridget's eyes returned to Brad. "Mr. Barkley is an exceptional principal. Everyone loves him."

Brad cleared his throat. "Our faculty works well as a team." The moment Brad led the way into the cafeteria, a middle-aged couple approached and pulled him aside.

Ashley leaned close to Jimmy, within earshot of Erica. "Is it my imagination, or does Bridget have the hots for your father?"

"You're not imagining it. Everyone, including Dad, knows that after her divorce, she set her sights on becoming the second Mrs. Brad Barkley."

"He is a great catch, especially for a middle-aged guy." Ashley faced Erica. "You don't need to worry about her. Brad displayed your picture, not hers, in his living room."

"Ashley's right. If he had the slightest interest in the woman, he would have made a move by now." Jimmy caught Erica's eye. "In case you're wondering, practically the entire town knows who you are and that you and Dad are dating."

Erica fidgeted. "How?"

Ashley chuckled. "Around here, going out to dinner nearly every week with the same guy either means you're married or in a serious relationship."

"So it seems." At least no one other than Amanda and Wendy knew about the black ring box.

Brad ambled back over and touched Erica's elbow. "We need to head to the food line before I'm cornered again." His voice rose barely above a whisper.

Students and parents interacted with the four of them the entire time they were in the cafeteria, clarifying Jimmy's comments. After finishing burgers, beans, and potato salad, they headed to the gym and sat at the reserved space behind the players' bench.

Moments before the game began, Bridget moseyed over and squeezed in between Erica and the woman Brad had introduced as the assistant principal. "Are you as much of a sports fan as our former football coach?"

Erica edged closer to Brad. *Could this woman be any more obvious?* "I enjoy sports, especially golf. Brad taught me how to play. Are you a golfer?"

Bridget's lips pursed. "I've never played, but I'm willing to learn."

Refusing to make eye contact, Erica laser focused on the court. Was Brad ignoring the woman, or was he too engrossed in the game to notice?

Five minutes after their team scored the first basket, Bridget moved to a different section of the bleachers.

Brad nudged Erica's arm. "Well done."

Feeling like a high school girl sitting beside the most popular boy in school, Erica smiled. He had noticed.

Following their team's decisive win, they returned to Brad's SUV. During the drive to Ashley and Jimmy's apartment, the guys discussed the game and the school's chances to make the playoffs. When he pulled up to the curve, Ashley leaned forward. "Tonight was fun. We should double date again."

Erica turned toward the back seat. "Great idea."

Jimmy stepped onto the sidewalk. Ashley slid across the seat and followed him. "We'll see you two later."

As soon as Jimmy closed the door, Brad pulled away from the curb.

Erica ran her fingers along her seatbelt. "You're one popular guy."

"Are you referring to students, teachers, or one over-zealous parent?"

"Bridget reminds me of Britany Livingston."

"Oh yeah." Brad stopped at a red light. "The young woman who believed she'd marry Chris. Until Wendy came to town."

Erica hesitated. Should she mention Bridget? Why not? "I assume you're aware that the over-zealous parent has her sights set on you."

"The woman isn't what you would call subtle. You're not worried about her, are you?"

Erica shrugged. "She's not your type, and she doesn't play golf."

"Two strikes against her." The light turned green. "Besides, I'm committed to a gorgeous brunette who has my engagement ring stashed away somewhere safe."

Erica stole a sideways glance at Brad's profile. He hadn't mentioned the ring since the night she halted his proposal. Was it her imagination, or did his tone hint of frustration?

Silence hung heavy until Brad parked on the ranch house driveway and walked Erica to the front door. She dug her keys from her purse. Would he kiss her? "I'm glad your team won tonight."

"They're good kids." He kissed her cheek without a hint of passion. "I'll call you tomorrow." He spun away and headed back to the driveway.

A sinking sensation invaded Erica's stomach as she unlocked the front door and stepped into the foyer. Grateful no one was in sight, she headed straight to her room. After peeling out of her coat, she eyed the dresser drawer concealing the black box. Despite his promise to give her all the time she needed, Erica sensed Brad's patience was beginning to wear thin.

Chapter 24

Amanda leaned close to the bathroom mirror and touched the skin under her right eye. If redheads tended to show their age more quickly than blondes or brunettes, how long before lines would appear around her eyes and mouth? Gary Redding was six years older than her, so what did it matter? Dismissing the thought as a ridiculous reaction to their board's chief information officer, Amanda finished applying makeup then returned to her room and eyed the bottle of perfume sitting on her dresser. The last time she'd spritzed fragrance on her neck, Paul Sullivan aka Gunter Benson shared her bed. Despite Millie's incessant badgering, her role as Awesam's president and Keith's campaign manager plus helping care for an infant made even the remote possibility of allowing another man in her life beyond ridiculous. Besides, she was perfectly happy being single.

Twenty minutes after stashing the perfume in a dresser drawer and heading out to the carport, Amanda turned into the Armstrong Law Firm parking lot, and chose the space beside Gary's late model sedan. He climbed out. She lifted her laptop and purse off the truck's passenger seat then met Keith's campaign finance manager on the sidewalk leading to the front door. "Our second official meeting."

"With more to come in the near future."

His smile and the way his blue eyes lit up the moment they met hers triggered a sensation Amanda hadn't experienced since she had lost the love of her life. Fearing her cheeks were seconds from turning a bright shade of pink, she broke eye contact. Had he noticed her reaction?

Gary held the door open for her.

Amanda's shoulder accidentally brushed his chest as she stepped into the reception area, sending a tingle racing through her limbs.

"Good morning." Linda moved from behind the receptionist's desk. "I'm filling in for Rosalie until she recovers from the flu, which is why we're meeting here." She led the way to the conference room and pointed to two chairs. "You two sit on that side."

Gary pulled the chair out for Amanda then settled beside her.

"Keith will join us in a few minutes." Linda sat across the table. "In the meantime, I have an idea to run by you. You're both articulate and quick on your feet—"

"Uh-oh." Gary chuckled. "Our campaign secretary is about to hit us with a questionable request."

"Questionable, no. Brilliant yes." Linda's focus shifted to Amanda, then back to Gary. "You two need to discuss our campaign on Nancy's Nuggets."

Gary scooted his chair closer to the table. "I assume that's some sort of podcast."

"Only the most popular in North Georgia. Nancy has interviewed Amanda twice, which makes our brilliant campaign manager a local celebrity."

Gary turned toward Amanda, grinning. "Our campaign manager is both famous and beautiful."

"Two interviews with my partners hardly qualifies me for celebrity status." Hoping to thwart the flush threatening to spread across her cheeks,

Amanda twisted the cap off a bottle of water and took a long sip. Had she turned into a silly teenager smitten by a good-looking guy?

Linda laced her fingers on the table. "I've already contacted Nancy. She agreed to interview you two as well as Keith in early spring."

Gary reached for a water bottle. "That gives Amanda and me plenty of time to prepare."

Keith ambled in and dropped beside Linda. "Our campaign is on the verge of erupting into a civil war. Rumor has it Richard Watson is digging up every scrap of gossip he can find about the four of us." Keith's eyes met Amanda's. "Including your relationship with Gunter Benson."

"In the event you're wondering where Keith and I stand, we've always known Watson would fight dirty." Linda leaned forward. "If you're comfortable with the potential fallout, we want you to stay on our team."

"Linda's right." Keith's eyes met Amanda's. "However, if you want to bow out, we'll understand."

Amanda's chest tightened. She should have known her past would creep into the campaign. "If you'll excuse me for a few minutes—" She pulled her phone from her purse. "I need to talk to my partners." Her pulse accelerated as she headed out to the hall that led to the reception area. Grateful she was alone, Amanda tapped her phone keypad and conferenced in Wendy, Erica, and Abby. "We have a problem." She relayed Keith's warning about the man who had deceived them. "I suppose we all knew we'd never be completely free of Gunter."

"You're not considering quitting the campaign, are you?" Wendy's tone hinted of surprise.

"Exposing you, Erica, and Abby to Watson's wrath is unfair."

"Chris and I have talked about the risk. No matter what happens, we're committed to support whatever decision you make a hundred percent."

"I appreciate your support, Wendy, but what about you, Erica?"

A long moment of silence lapsed before she spoke. "That day I sat in the Las Vegas witness stand and faced the man who had taken so much from us, I vowed never to let him intimidate me again."

Amanda peered out the front window. Gunter's truck parked beside Gary's car seemed to mock her. "You understand the truth about his illegal marriages to Wendy, you, and me will likely become public."

"Do you remember what Gail Weston wrote about the three of us last spring?" asked Erica.

Amanda's mind drifted to the newspaper article the freelance reporter had created. "That we rejected victimhood and its limitations to take charge of our lives and embrace new possibilities?"

"Exactly. Which we have been doing for the past thirteen months."

"I know how much you dislike confrontation, Erica—"

"I'm tougher than you realize. Besides, the most important people in my life already know about my past."

Amanda turned away from the window. "This also affects you, Abby."

"Back in Asheville I survived bullies and my best friend abandoning me. Like Mom said, the most important people in our lives already know about Gunter. So, I vote you stay with the campaign and defeat the jerk district attorney. Especially after he tried to put Jimmy Barkley in jail."

"Speaking for Erica and Abby, the three of us appreciate you asking for our approval, Amanda. However, the decision is yours."

Amanda ambled to the receptionist's desk. "Your support means the world to me."

"Then you're staying?" asked Wendy.

"The jury's still out." Amanda ended the call. There was one more person whose reputation was at risk. She returned to the conference room.

Gary stood and pulled Amanda's chair out for her.

She sat and scooted close to the table. "Before I decide what to do—" Amanda faced Gary. "I need to know what you know about Gunter Benson."

He shrugged. "Other than you were somehow related to him, nothing. Why does he matter?"

"You need to know what Watson will use in an attempt to damage my reputation." Amanda hesitated. If she dropped out of the campaign, her integrity wouldn't be jeopardized. Her jaw clenched. If her partners were willing to take the risk, so should she. "Before Gunter was found guilty of murder, he was also known as Paul Sullivan, Brian Parker, and Kurt Peterson." She paused. "When I moved here from New Orleans, my last name was Sullivan."

Gary turned his shoulders toward Amanda. "Did you know he was a criminal when you married him?"

Amanda shook her head. "If I'd had the slightest inkling, I'd never have accepted his proposal."

"Then what's the big deal?"

"There's more to the story." Amanda breathed deeply, then slowly released the air. "Two of my business partners and I were married to him...at the same time."

Gary's gaze softened then probed. "You're worried about a scandal, aren't you?"

"Blue Ridge is a small town—"

"And Richard Watson is a crooked district attorney. I understand if you need to walk away from the campaign to protect yourself and your partners."

"The four of us are willing to take the risk. What about you?"

Gary's eyes remained trained on Amanda. "You know I'm divorced, right?"

Amanda nodded.

"What you don't know is my marriage ended following a scandal my wife and one of my bank employees caused when they began an affair. Watson, who was in private practice, represented my ex and lost. You can bet he'll bring up that whole mess." Gary touched Amanda's arm. "Believe me, the four of us in this room have a lot more friends in this town than Watson has." A warm smile softened Gary's features. "If you're wondering whether or not I want you to stay on the good guys' team, the answer is yes."

Was his response based on personal or professional interest in her? Did his reason matter? "All right then." Amanda faced Keith and Linda. "There's no way I'll let two scumbags force me off the winning team."

Linda's face lit up. "Richard Watson has no idea what he's up against."

Chapter 25

After laying her little guy in his crib for his afternoon nap, Wendy traipsed across the hall to the home office she shared with Chris. Duke sprawled on the floor beside her as she settled at her desk and opened her laptop to her current college course. Another month and she'd complete her fifth quarter toward an online degree. One day she would encourage her partners to expand their business beyond Hilltop Inn. Maybe they could open a restaurant or another bed and breakfast. A smile curled her lips. Awesam could become a conglomerate.

Kayla's ringtone disrupted Wendy's musing. She pressed FaceTime and peered at her sister's red nose and watery eyes. "Have you been crying?"

She shook her head. "Bad cold. I caught it from my sister. She's also home from school." Kayla sneezed. "At least I have a couple more days to study before taking a makeup algebra test."

"Are you finally taking math seriously?"

"Not really." Kayla blew her nose. "Mom's staying with her best friend for a few days. You know what that means, don't you?"

Wendy nodded. "She doesn't want to catch your germs."

"Or because she's already sick."

"Are you guessing, or did your parents clue you in?"

"No one's told me anything." Another sneeze. "Spring break is next week. Dad's taking us to Dollywood."

"Including your mother?"

"Yeah."

Was it possible her sister was wrong about her mother's health? "Given she's well enough to travel, chances are Cynthia's recovering from whatever's been ailing her."

Kayla's brow pinched then released. "She has seemed a lot better these past few days."

"Well, there you go."

"Guess it's okay to stop worrying."

"Good idea."

"At least until after our trip." Kayla fell silent for a long moment. "Is my nephew awake?"

Wendy eyed the photo on the corner of her desk—Ryan sitting on Chris's lap. "He's taking a nap."

"When he wakes up, give him a hug for me." Kayla's hand covered the phone for a brief moment. "My sister just walked in. We'll talk later."

"Take care of yourself, and get well soon."

"Okay." Kayla ended the call.

Wendy sighed. Would she ever have the opportunity to meet her other siblings? Her focus returned to the online course. An hour passed before her phone rang a second time. She glanced at the name, then swiped her finger across the screen and pressed speaker. "Hey, Donna."

"Is this a good time to talk?"

Odd her secret sister and her secret stepmother would call within an hour of each other. "Perfect time for a break. What's up?"

"Thanks for texting the latest pictures of Ryan."

"You're welcome. I'll send more tomorrow."

"How's everything going with Chris?"

"He's busy working on a new case."

"Any unusual guests at Hilltop Inn?"

Wendy raised a brow. Had Donna called to chitchat, or was she stalling before sharing the real reason for the call? "Not that I know of."

A long moment of silence. "My mother and her husband are missionaries in a South American jungle. I haven't spoken to my father since I was eighteen, and my brother is on an aircraft carrier halfway across the globe." Donna paused.

What was her stepmother really trying to tell her? Wendy pushed away from the desk. "I imagine a lot of families are scattered about." She crossed the hall and peeked into Ryan's room. Still asleep.

"The Hewitts all protect each other for the sake of their business empire." Donna's tone mocked.

"In a way that makes sense." Wendy pulled the door closed then headed to the great room.

"The fact is, you're my only family member I can confide in."

And there it was. The real reason for the call. "What's going on?"

A sigh resonated. "Whether women are willing to face the truth or choose to ignore the signs, wives know when their husbands are cheating on them." Another long pause. "Especially when their latest honey shows up at his front door."

Wendy's eyes widened. "Are you serious?"

"Yesterday morning. She informed me that my husband was in love with her."

"Talk about a foolish move."

"Not only was she young enough to be Douglas's daughter, but she also had no idea that affairs with men like him are based on lies."

Wendy dropped onto the sofa. "What did you do?"

"Like a good mother, I invited her in to prove I wasn't the cold, heartless wife Douglas made me out to be."

"Bet she was surprised to learn the truth."

"Surprised is an understatement. Especially when I enlightened her about all of her lover's other affairs."

Duke padded into the great room and plopped his head on Wendy's lap, prompting her to stroke his muzzle. "How'd she react?"

"She cried. I suspect as much from humiliation as from anger."

Wendy's shoulders tensed as her mind drifted to the moment she accepted the fact that the man she had known as Kurt Peterson was a con man named Gunter Benson. "Discovering you've been deceived by someone you love unleashes all sorts of heartbreaking emotions."

"The second my husband's lover stepped into my home, something compelled me to begin recording our conversation. Secretly, of course."

"Self-preservation."

Donna remained silent for a long moment. "After she left, I accepted the fact that my silence was no longer prudent." Another long pause. "Late last night I gathered the courage to share the recording with Douglas."

"Bet he was shocked."

"Especially when I told him he needed to move out to protect our sons."

"Did he agree?"

"I didn't give him a choice—either he leaves, or I share the recording with our boys."

"Good for you."

"This morning before our sons left for school, we joined forces and explained that although their dad and I loved them, we needed time apart."

"How did they take the news?"

"It's curious. They were sad, but they didn't seem all that surprised."

Kayla's suspicions about her mother's health played in Wendy's mind. "Children, especially teenagers, are more aware of what's going on than their parents sometimes realize."

"At least we protected them from their father's infidelity."

Wendy tucked her ankle under her knee. "How are you holding up?"

"After I invited my husband's flavor of the month into our home, the more details I shared, the more I blamed myself."

"Douglas's cheating wasn't your fault."

"Intellectually, I understand." Donna released a heavy sigh. "Emotionally, I can't help but wonder what would have happened if I had confronted him when I first learned of his affairs."

"Believe me, some men don't have the will or humility to change, unless some sort of trauma scares them straight."

Donna remained silent for another long moment, as if considering Wendy's comment. "Other than someone threatening his sons, I can't imagine anything intimidating Douglas."

"Like telling them the truth about their father's extracurricular activities?"

"Exactly." Their conversation continued for half an hour before Donna ended the call with a promise to keep Wendy updated.

After pocketing her phone, Wendy returned to her desk. Following a futile attempt to concentrate on her class, she eased into Ryan's room. Duke followed and sprawled on the floor beside the crib. Wendy pressed her hand to her heart as she peered at her sleeping child. Her little guy was blessed to have Chris as his daddy—a father he could admire and emulate. Wendy's brows snapped together. Who would teach Donna's sons, her half-brothers, how to become honorable men who respected women?

Chapter 26

Following a deep-tissue massage for a chatty hotel guest, Erica locked her office, returned to the ranch house, and removed a protein shake from the fridge. She poured the liquid into a glass then meandered into the den and sat across the table from Awesam's president. "Anything exciting going on?"

"You tell me." Amanda turned her laptop around.

"Wow." Erica's eyes widened as she stared at the GoFundMe page. "Our Little Pip has obviously captured a lot of hearts."

Amanda nodded. "Now that we have enough money to cover Theo's surgery, we should shut the fundraiser down."

"That's one option." Erica took a sip of her protein drink. "The other is to keep it running until after the surgery to cover any unexpected expenses."

"Good idea." Amanda responded to her ringing phone with a finger swipe. "Hey, Keith, what's up?" She pushed away from the table and headed to the hall.

Erica let Dusty in from the backyard, then carried her drink to the sofa and clicked on the television to catch up on the latest news.

Ten minutes later, Amanda ambled in carrying wide-awake Theo. "That didn't take long." Her hardened expression spoke volumes.

Erica muted the television. "What's going on?"

"DA Watson threatened to expose the truth about Gunter if Keith doesn't withdraw from the race."

"We all knew he'd play dirty." Erica stared wide eyed at Amanda. "Keith didn't capitulate, did he?"

Amanda settled beside Erica. "He offered to. I called Wendy. She's ready to deal with the gossip." She reached across the cushion and touched Erica's arm. "I want to make sure you're still okay with the truth coming out."

"I refuse to allow men like Richard Watson and Gunter Benson to intimidate me."

"Good, because Keith, Gary, and I are scheduled for a Nancy's Nuggets interview tomorrow to beat him at his own game. By the end of the day, at least a thousand people will know the truth."

"That number will increase at least threefold by the end of the week." Responding to Abby's ringtone, Erica pulled her phone from her pocket and pressed the speaker. "Hey, sweetheart."

"Are you busy? Is Theo awake?"

"No, I'm not busy, and yes, he's awake. What's up?"

"Everyone's asking how he's doing, so I'm thinking maybe you should bring him to the crisis center."

"When?"

"Now, if you don't mind."

Why not? Especially since she had news to share with her daughter. "I'll be there shortly."

"Thanks, Mom."

After packing a diaper bag, Erica secured Little Pip in his car seat and backed onto the street. How should she tell Abby about the DA's threat? Even though her daughter had claimed she could handle any sort of scandal, would she have second thoughts now that the truth was a little more than twenty-four hours from becoming public knowledge? By the time Erica pulled into the crisis center parking lot, her mouth was dry and her palms damp. She removed the carrier from the base, then grabbed the diaper bag, headed to the front door, and pressed the buzzer.

"Is that you, Mom?" Abby's voice came through loud and clear.

"In the flesh."

The door swung open. Erica stepped inside and closed the door, then released Theo from the carrier and placed him in her daughter's arms.

Abby cradled the child. "Are you ready to meet some fans?"

Erica set the carrier aside before pushing Abby's wheelchair down the hall to the large eat-in kitchen. Four mothers and seven children sat around two tables eating lunch. Lucky, the center's comfort dog, sprawled on the floor between the tables.

"Hey everyone, come meet Theo."

Five of the children rushed to gather around Abby. The youngest girl pointed. "He looks kinda funny."

A young boy leaned close. "What's wrong with his mouth?"

"Good question, Matthew." Abby peered at the child. "Theo was born with what's called a cleft lip. In a few weeks doctors will fix his mouth, so he looks like all of us."

Matthew patted Theo's head. "Are they gonna glue the two halves together?"

An older girl ambled over. "That's a stupid question," her tone mocked.

Abby faced the girl. "He asked a good question, Evie. In fact, sometimes doctors use special glue instead of stitches."

Evie's eyes widened. "Really?"

"Uh-huh."

Evie twirled a lock of hair around her finger. "Is Theo your and Tommy's baby?"

Erica stared at the girl.

Abby smiled. "No, but Mom and I are helping take care of him until someone adopts him."

Evie's head tilted. "Why don't you adopt him?"

"Sorry." Evie's mother ambled over. "My daughter is more than a little inquisitive."

"It's okay. Like Matthew, Evie also asked a legitimate question." Theo's face scrunched seconds before he emitted his 'I'm hungry' cry. "Do you want to see the special way we give him his bottle?"

Heads nodded. The children remained gathered around Abby while she demonstrated how to feed a cleft-lip infant.

Erica returned to the reception area to retrieve the carrier. Why hadn't Abby answered the question about her adopting Theo? Would she explain after she finished feeding him?

Moments after Theo finished his bottle, Abby supported him on her shoulder and patted his back. The girl who had asked about her adopting Theo cocked her head to the side. "Mommy used to do that to my little brother to make him burp."

One of the boys grinned. "Like this?" He released a loud belch.

The girl nodded. "Uh-huh."

The boy's mother, whose black eye had turned into shades of green and yellow, frowned. "It's not polite to burp in public, Joey."

Abby faced the child. "Your mother's right."

"Why not? Daddy did it all the time."

A middle-aged woman strode in, smiling. "Are you children ready for today's class?"

The girl who had claimed Theo looked funny peered up at the center's newest volunteer. "Are you gonna read to us, Ms. Patti?"

"After our lessons, sweetie."

Ms. Patti and Burping Boy's mother, who had volunteered to help with the lessons, led the children from the kitchen to the center's classroom. The other mothers remained to clean up as Lucky padded behind the kids. After her mother placed Theo in his carrier, Abby motioned for her to follow her. Inside her office, she maneuvered her chair beside her desk. "Thank you for bringing Theo."

Her mom placed the carrier on the loveseat then settled on the cushion beside him. "I enjoyed watching the children's reactions." Her eyes met Abby's. "I'm curious. Did you intentionally avoid answering Evie's question about adopting Theo?"

Abby's focus shifted to Theo. How could anyone understand the connection she felt for the infant she had rescued? Had her dream about becoming Theo's mother been triggered by an unrealistic desire or some sort of premonition? She blinked. As close as she was to her own mother, she couldn't share what she failed to understand. "Theo obviously distracted me." Abby shrugged. "By now Evie has forgotten she asked, which lets me off the hook until she comes up with another intriguing question."

The crisis center's director tapped on Abby's door. "A deputy is bringing a woman and her teenaged daughter over from the hospital. They'll stay with us until the sheriff's department finds and arrests the live-in boyfriend who beat her up and took off in her car. According to the deputy, the daughter is terrified the guy will kill her mother. I'll need you in the reception area in five minutes." The director spun around and headed down the hall.

Exchanging a knowing glance with her mom, Abby remembered her prayer the day she blew out the seven candles on her birthday cake with the wish that her daddy wouldn't kill her mommy.

Abby's mother reached for her hand. "No one understands what that troubled young girl needs more than you do. I'll take care of Theo while you go fulfill the role you've been called to."

"I love you, Mom."

"I love you too, and couldn't be prouder of you, sweetheart."

Chapter 27

With dark clouds threatening rain rolling in from the west, Amanda quickly slid onto the front passenger seat beside Keith in his late-model luxury sedan. She buckled her seat belt while Gary climbed in behind him. During the past two and a half hours, Linda had played the role of interviewer to prepare the three of them for today's podcast. Amanda glanced at her watch. In thirty minutes there would be no turning back from the realities of a political campaign against a corrupt candidate who would stoop to any level to keep his job. She breathed deeply to slow her racing pulse as Keith backed out and turned toward McCaysville. The three-member team remained silent, each seemingly lost in their own thoughts.

Amanda dismissed the weather as a harbinger of the days ahead and focused on the passing scenery. A deer grazing at the edge of the woods looked up as they drove past. Despite Blue Ridge's destination as a popular tourist attraction, North Georgia was a lot different than life had been in New Orleans. Rolling hills. No hurricanes threatening to inundate the city with rising floodwater. Far less crime. She stole a quick glance at Keith's profile. A successful election bode well for the future district attorney who had survived a serious heart attack five years earlier. During the remainder of the drive, Amanda leaned her head back, closed her eyes, and summoned happy memories.

"We're here."

Amanda's eyes popped open as Keith turned onto the driveway beside Nancy's two-story frame house. After cutting the engine, he glanced at Amanda then Gary. "Are you two ready?"

Amanda nodded. "Ready."

"And eager," added Gary.

"All right then." Keith opened his door. "Time to shift our campaign into high gear."

Amanda shouldered her purse then caught up with the men on the front sidewalk.

Their interviewer met them at the front door. "Welcome, I'm Nancy Campbell." She extended her hand to Keith, then to Gary. "You're my first political interview."

Keith smiled. "Given this is Gary and my inaugural podcast experience, today is a first for three of us."

Nancy escorted them into a familiar room off the foyer. With two podcasts under Amanda's belt, at least for the moment, she was the most experienced member of the Keith Armstrong campaign team. Following their host's instructions, she sat in front of the middle microphone with Keith on her left and Gary on her right. Amanda grabbed a bottle of water off the table, twisted off the cap, and swallowed a mouthful.

Nancy took her place at the head of the table. "Given this is your first podcast, all you need to do during our interview is relax and treat this as a casual conversation among friends."

"Seems easy enough." Gary's tone came across as confident.

"Do you gentlemen need a quick practice round?"

Keith folded his arms on the table. "We appreciate the offer; however, we're ready without a rehearsal."

"Excellent. I'll address my questions to you by name or by eye contact. When you answer, speak directly into the mike." Five minutes after a mike check, Nancy counted down from three then leaned close to her microphone. "Good afternoon, friends, and welcome to Nancy's Nuggets. Today we'll hear from Mr. Keith Armstrong, candidate for our area's district attorney, along with his campaign manager, Amanda Smith, and finance manager, Gary Redding. Mr. Armstrong, tell our audience what compelled you to leave a thriving law practice founded by your father to run for political office."

Keith squared his shoulders, obviously ready with his rehearsed response. "For many of us, there comes a time in our careers when we are called to a higher purpose. For me that calling is to bring my experience and expertise to our judicial district."

"What distinctions do you draw between yourself and the current DA?"

Amanda's shoulders tensed. Another question they'd anticipated, this one guaranteed to rile their opponent.

"Three key factors are critical to this race. First, I have fifteen more years of legal experience than my opponent. Second, I understand that every district attorney is elected to serve their constituents." He paused for a brief moment. "Third, and most importantly, I pledge to bring integrity and impartiality to the office."

"Are you insinuating the current district attorney lacks those principles?"

"Given my firm's experiences as well as recent threats, I'm stating the facts."

Nancy's brows raised. "What sort of threats?"

"Threatening to spread gossip about my staff unless I drop out of the race. Based on our commitment to honesty, we've chosen to share those details with the public."

Amanda leaned forward. "Beginning with me. The first time I was a guest on your podcast, my business partners and I shared how we met during last year's blizzard and discovered a man named Gunter Benson had stolen everything from us." Amanda paused.

Nancy's eyes met hers. "There's more to the story, isn't there?"

"Yes. What we didn't reveal is that Gunter was also known as Paul Sullivan, Brian Parker, and Kurt Peterson." The next words stuck in Amanda's throat as if she had swallowed a giant jawbreaker.

Nancy eyed her. "How is that information relevant to the campaign?"

The walls seemed to close in on Amanda. Would her Awesam family survive the gossip she was seconds from revealing? Would their new friends blame them for not realizing they had married a fraud? Gary touched her arm. She blinked and dug deep for the courage to continue. "The first day the three of us checked into Blue Ridge Inn...Erica expected her husband, Brian, to arrive. Wendy expected her husband, Kurt, and I expected my husband, Paul."

Nancy's eyes widened. "Are you saying all three of you were married to the man whose real name was Gunter Benson?"

"Yes." Amanda imagined a collective gasp emanating among the podcast audience.

Nancy's eyes remained laser focused on Amanda. "You and your partners refused to become victims, moved to Blue Ridge, and paid the back taxes on the Harrington properties, didn't you?"

Grateful Nancy remembered, Amanda squared her shoulders. "We chose to take control of our lives." She stole a quick glance at Keith. "My partners and I refuse to allow our past to prevent an honorable man from becoming our next district attorney."

"Mr. Armstrong, were you aware of the situation when you recruited Amanda as your campaign manager?"

"Yes. We understood the risk. At the same time, Amanda and Gary's business and organizational skills are vital to my campaign."

"Something else the public needs to know." Gary leaned forward. "During our drive from Blue Ridge, I received an anonymous text threatening to dredge up details about my divorce if I didn't convince Mr. Armstrong to withdraw as a candidate." He paused for a brief moment.

Amanda stared wide-eyed at their finance manager before turning toward Keith. His expression made it clear the news had also blindsided him. Had Gary failed to tell them before they walked in, fearing they'd back out of the interview?

"The three of us refuse to allow threats to stop us, which is why I'm ready to reveal the facts myself." Gary's tone remained calm. "Three days after my wife and I celebrated our tenth anniversary, I discovered she and our bank's assistant manager had been involved in a six-month-long affair. I fired him and filed for divorce. My wife initiated a lawsuit, claiming I had cheated on her with a close family friend and driven her into the arms of the other man. When her accusations were proven false, she and her lover left Blue Ridge. Although I haven't spoken to either of them since, I hope they're happy."

"You're a true gentleman, sir." Nancy laced her fingers on the table. "Now that your team has trusted voters with the truth, tell us your plans as our next district attorney, Mr. Armstrong."

Following an hour-long conversation, Nancy ended the podcast with a promise to bring the team back for another interview. She switched off the microphones and escorted them to the front door. "Although I can't publicly endorse you, I guarantee that you have *my* vote."

Outside, the dark clouds had passed on by without releasing a drop of rain. Gary opened the front passenger door for Amanda. Moments after buckling her seatbelt, she pulled her pinging phone from her purse. A text from Wendy. "Well done, partner." A second text from Erica. "I'm proud of you." After responding to both messages with heart and thumbs-up emojis, Amanda dropped her phone into her purse, then leaned back, smiling. Once again she and her Awesam family had faced adversity and refused to become victims.

Chapter 28

Six weeks had passed since the podcast, and now the morning eased toward dawn. Erica tossed her coat over the den sofa then followed the scent of freshly brewed coffee to the kitchen. After filling a mug and adding creamer and sugar, she returned to the den and settled at the dining room table across from Amanda. "Today's a big day."

"In more ways than one." Amanda tapped her laptop screen. "Theo's GoFundMe is still growing."

"Seems Blue Ridge's collective heart has embraced Little Pip."

Abby rolled her wheelchair beside Erica, Theo's carrier balanced on her lap. "He's ready for his miracle transformation."

Erica reached into the carrier and touched the infant's cheek. "Tomorrow morning you'll wake up more handsome than ever." He rewarded her with a smile. "You know you're adorable, don't you."

Amanda pushed away from the table. "I'll warm up the car and meet you at the end of the sidewalk in five." She grabbed her coat off the chair and headed to the back door.

Abby stretched a stocking cap on Theo. "I promised everyone at the crisis center I'd bring him back as soon as he heals."

"Based on social media comments, half the town is waiting for updated photos."

"We should throw him a big party."

"If he's still with us when he turns one." Erica took another sip of coffee, then slipped into her coat, lifted the carrier off her daughter's lap, and headed out the front door. Her daughter followed close behind.

Amanda held the passenger door open for Abby, then stowed her wheelchair in the trunk while Erica secured the carrier in its base and climbed in beside Theo. By the time they pulled into the hospital parking lot, the sun had crept over the horizon.

Chris's sister met them in the lobby. "He's all checked in."

"It helps to have a doctor in the family." After Erica placed Theo in Allison's arms, the trio followed her to the surgical wing where a nurse took charge of the patient.

Abby's eyes seemed to follow the nurse as she pressed a button before disappearing into a restricted area. "He's so tiny and helpless," Abby's voice quivered.

Allison placed her hand on Abby's shoulder. "Not only is Theo a healthy baby, his surgeon is one of the best in Georgia."

Abby spun her wheelchair away from the closed double doors. "That doesn't make this any easier."

"Time seems to slow to a crawl when we're waiting without knowing what's happening." Allison settled on a chair in the waiting area across from Erica. "When Dad had his heart attack, I was a resident in a big-city hospital, and Chris was in his final weeks of law school. That drive back to Blue Ridge was the longest in my life. Fortunately, by the time we both arrived back in town, Dad was out of danger."

Amanda sat beside Erica. "It's amazing how healthy Keith is now."

"Thanks to Mom and Grandma Susan forcing him to rest. That scare is also the reason Chris turned down a position in a prestigious Atlanta law firm and moved back to Blue Ridge. In the long run, it turned out to be a good decision, especially after he met Wendy."

Abby's head tilted. "It's funny how bad experiences sometimes turn out good. I never would have considered working at the crisis center if Mom and I hadn't spent time in a Baltimore women's shelter all those years ago." Her eyes met Erica's. "If you hadn't married the man you thought was Brian Parker, you'd still be working part-time jobs in Asheville, and I'd be going to some fancy college on a ton of borrowed money. Instead we're both successful career women doing what we love. Which means I'm off the hook, right, Mom?"

Erica flashed a smile at her daughter. "Absolutely."

Allison's focus shifted from Erica to Abby. "Off the hook for what?"

"When Mom and I lived in a cramped apartment, I dreamed of living in a nice house with a normal family, like my two best friends' families. After Mom started dating Brian aka Gunter, I sort of begged her for a new daddy."

"To be honest—" Erica hesitated, brushing her fingers through her hair. "—even if Abby hadn't made that comment, I would have married him for the lifestyle he could give us."

Abby stared wide-eyed. "You never told me that before."

"It's taken me a long time to admit the truth to myself."

Amanda exhaled. "Given our venture into true confessions, I'll admit I was also attracted by the financial stability Paul aka Gunter could provide for Morgan and me. Strange how even after we married and moved into his million-plus-dollar house on St. Charles, she never warmed up to him. Turns out my daughter was right not to trust the con man."

Allison crossed one leg over the other. "Although my stories aren't as dramatic as yours, I also experienced some relationship drama. During my first year in medical school, I fell madly in love with a fellow student. In addition to being movie-star handsome, he drove a red Ferrari, which for a small-town girl was more than a little exciting. We dated for seven months before he was expelled for cheating on a final exam. When I came home during spring break, I reconnected with Mark. Fourteen months later we married." Allison's lips curved into a smile. "Turns out my high school sweetheart is one of the good guys as well as my soulmate."

Erica stroked her naked left ring finger. How would Abby react if she knew about the black box hidden in her dresser drawer? Especially since she thought the world of Brad. Erica caught Amanda staring at her. Had her partner somehow read her mind? She blinked as Ms. Abernathy from Child Services strolled in carrying a box of donuts and napkins.

"Good morning, ladies."

Allison faced her. "Hey, Jillian."

She handed the box and napkins to her friend. "Any word on Theo?"

"Not yet." Allison opened the box and selected a donut then passed it along with the remaining napkins to Erica.

She eyed the assortment, opting for one with chocolate icing and sprinkles. Should she address the gift bearer as Jillian or as Ms. Abernathy? Neither to be safe. "Thank you for the donuts."

"You're welcome."

Erica passed the treat to Abby.

"The entire town is eager for an update on Theo." Jillian sat across from Erica and Amanda. "I assume you ladies are aware you've become local heroes."

Erica raised a brow. "For helping Theo?"

"Yes." Jillian's eyes shifted from Erica to Amanda. "Also because you revealed details about the depth of Gunter Benson's deception. Everyone understands how much courage it took to be that vulnerable."

Abby swallowed a bite of donut before wiping her fingers with a napkin. "My mother, Amanda, and Wendy are perfect role models for every girl and woman who comes face-to-face with a bully."

"So are you for standing up to your snooty high school friends after they turned on you, sweetheart."

A smile lit Abby's face. "Now I have genuine friends."

Jillian nodded. "Family and friends who stand by you no matter what happens make all the difference."

Twenty minutes after Jillian arrived, all eyes turned toward a thin young woman shuffling in from the hall wearing a stocking hat, jeans, and an oversized sweatshirt.

Allison stood. "I'm Dr. Baker. How can I help you?"

"I...um...was kinda wondering how the baby's doing."

"We're all waiting to hear." Allison motioned to her chair then glanced at her watch. "You can have my seat."

The young woman's chin dipped to her chest as she dropped onto the chair.

"My first patient is due at my office in twenty minutes. Text me after you talk to the surgeon, and I'll forward the message to the rest of our family."

Erica peered up at Allison. "We will."

Moments after Allison walked away, Abby moved close to the new arrival. "Two donuts are left." She handed over the box and the last napkin to the woman who appeared to be the same age as Abby.

The timid newcomer accepted the box. She hesitated, as if considering what to do next.

Abby leaned forward. "Go ahead, we've all had our share."

"Thanks." She pulled off her stocking hat then lifted a donut and took a bite.

Abby blinked. "What's your name?"

The young woman swallowed. "Sierra." She returned the box back to Abby.

Abby's eyes remained focused on the stranger. "Do you live in Blue Ridge?"

Sierra shook her head. "In Morganton. With my grandma."

Jillian's forehead creased. "You were here a couple of days after Theo was first brought in, weren't you?"

Sierra cut a quick glance at Jillian. "I was kinda curious after reading the GoFundMe page." She took the last bite of donut.

Amanda's pinging phone disrupted her curiosity about the young woman sitting across from her. She swiped the screen then stepped into the hall and smiled at her daughter. "We're still waiting."

"How's everyone holding up?"

"Okay, thanks to Allison's company, and Jillian, our Child Services friend, bringing donuts."

"Hopefully all the publicity will encourage a nice couple to adopt Theo, at which point you'd have to come up with a different nickname."

"Little Pip is such a fun name." Amanda's focus drifted to Sierra picking at her cuticle. She didn't appear to be out of her teens. Was it possible...

"Call me when you have an update, Mom."

"I will." Amanda pocketed her phone and returned to her chair. Her eyes remained focused on the newcomer's thin frame. Although she likely didn't weigh much more than a hundred pounds, she appeared healthy. Two rings adorned her left hand and three her right. Other than her ears, she had no other visible piercings. Who was this girl? "What's your last name, Sierra?"

Her chin remained dipped toward her chest. "Wellington."

"Are you from Morganton?"

She shook her head. "Chattanooga."

All eyes turned toward the double doors swinging open. Amanda, Erica, and Sierra stood the moment the man dressed in scrubs approached.

He introduced himself as the surgeon. "Theo is in recovery and doing well." He explained the surgical procedure and follow-up care. "You'll be able to see him as soon as we move him to the nursery."

Abby peered up at the doctor. "When can we take him home?"

"Tomorrow, after I examine him."

Moments after the surgeon left them alone, Sierra dropped onto the chair.

Unable to ignore her suspicions, Amanda sat beside her. "You're Theo's mother, aren't you?"

The young woman buried her face in her hands and wept.

An hour after seeing Theo's new face, Abby maneuvered onto her car's front seat and buckled her belt while Amanda slid behind the wheel. After stashing her wheelchair in the trunk, her mother climbed in behind the driver's seat. Abby's shoulders tensed as they backed out of the parking space and waited for Sierra's pickup to pull up behind them.

Amanda peered in the rearview mirror, her brows drawn together. "She hasn't uttered a word since admitting she was Theo's mother. What makes you think she'll talk now?"

Good question. Abby glanced over her shoulder. How would her mother respond?

She shrugged. "Why else would she have accepted my invitation to come to lunch?"

Amanda scoffed. "Morbid curiosity? Or maybe she wants a free meal."

Abby cringed. "What if she wants Theo back?"

"Doesn't matter." Amanda pulled out of the parking lot with Sierra trailing behind, followed by Ms. Abernathy's car. "I can't imagine Child Services granting her custody."

"I can't help feeling sorry for her."

Abby stole a quick glance at her mom. Feeling sorry for Theo's mother was one thing. Inviting her to their house seemed irresponsible. Especially since they didn't know anything about her.

"I suppose we all feel compassion for her." Amanda stopped at a red light. "However, empathy doesn't change the fact that Theo's mother dumped him on a doorstep in the middle of winter."

Exactly. Desperate to control her emotions, Abby pressed her earbuds into her ears and activated her play list. She stared blindly at the passing scenery until Amanda parked in the ranch house driveway. After her mother positioned her wheelchair beside her door, Abby lifted her body onto her ride and wheeled to the front door.

Millie met them in the foyer with her hands propped on her hips. She eyed Theo's mother from head to toe. "How old are you and why did you abandon your baby?"

Sierra's chin dropped to her chest.

"For goodness sake, Millie." Abby's mom's tone scolded. "Sierra's our guest."

"Guest or not. I'm Awesam's chief information officer, and she needs to answer a lot of questions."

Sierra lifted her chin. "I'm eighteen." Her voice was barely above a whisper.

"Good start. You can tell us more during lunch." Millie lowered her hands then led the way to the dining room table laden with sandwiches, fresh-baked cookies, and glasses of lemonade.

Abby positioned her chair between her mother and Amanda. Sierra squeezed in between Millie and Ms. Abernathy.

Following a short blessing, Erica handed the platter to Abby.

Millie folded her napkin in her lap. "Did you take pictures of Theo?"

"Lots of pictures." After giving the platter to Amanda, Abby pulled her phone from her pocket. She tapped the screen then handed it over.

Millie's mouth curved into a smile. "Little Pip is more adorable than ever."

Sierra stared at Millie. "His name's Theo."

Amanda reached for her lemonade. "Little Pip is his nickname."

Sierra's eyes shifted to Amanda. "Why?"

"Did you ever read *Great Expectations*?"

Theo's mother shook her head.

Abby peered at Millie's pursed lips. Was she seconds from explaining?

"Delicious sandwiches, Millie."

"My favorite egg salad recipe."

Abby's eyes shifted from their chef to her mother. Had she diverted the conversation to keep from embarrassing Sierra, or to avoid a confrontation between Amanda and Millie? If she revealed Little Pip as an orphan, would she come across as spiteful?

Ms. Abernathy shifted the conversation to favorite cookie flavors, making it clear the discussion about Theo's nickname was off the table. Moments after finishing her sandwich, the Crisis Center caseworker pushed her plate away and peered at Sierra. "The time has come for you to answer the second question Millie asked when we first arrived. Why did you abandon your baby, and why did you accept Erica's invitation to lunch?" Her tone was firm, almost accusatory.

Sierra's body seemed to stiffen. "I knew I couldn't take care of a sick baby. Now that I know he's okay..." She paused, her gaze darting from one to the other.

Abby cringed. How would Ms. Abernathy react if Theo's mother was seconds away from declaring she wanted him back? Sierra's eyes met Abby's. She held her breath.

Sierra blinked then looked away. "I just wanted to see his new home."

Abby released the air from her lungs.

Ms. Abernathy unfolded her arms. "You can rest assured these ladies are taking excellent care of Theo."

Relieved Ms. Abernathy hadn't referred to Little Pip as Sierra's son, Abby eyed the woman who had abandoned her baby. "You were smart to leave him at the crisis center."

"I know." Sierra pushed away from the table. "I'm ready to leave now."

Ms. Abernathy stood. "I'll walk you out."

Seconds after the front door opened then closed, Millie drummed her fingers on the table. "If you ask me, that girl is up to something."

"You can stop playing detective, Millie." Abby's mom laid her napkin on the table. "Jillian will keep us informed."

Millie's brow pinched. "Who's Jillian?"

"Ms. Abernathy."

"Oh. I still don't trust her."

Amanda pulled her phone from her pocket. "It's Wendy." She swiped her finger across the screen then set it on the table. "Hey, you're on speaker." Amanda relayed what had happened after they left the hospital. "Hold on, Jillian just walked back in."

Their Child Services contact returned to her chair and scanned the faces staring at her. "I suspect you're all wondering if Theo's mother has an ulterior motive."

Millie scoffed. "Don't you?"

Abby's back stiffened.

Ms. Abernathy wrapped her fingers around her glass. "In my opinion, Sierra has been experiencing guilt over abandoning her baby. Now after meeting all of you, she seems ready to move on with her life."

Abby's eyes met hers. "With or without Theo?"

"Based on her body language, I'd say without."

Chapter 29

Two weeks after Theo's surgery, Erica laid her fork across her plate and peered out the window at the building across the side street from Harvest on Main. Every date with Brad since they'd attended the high school basketball game with Jimmy and Ashley seemed more akin to a couple of friends catching up on the latest news than a rendezvous between an almost engaged couple. Thus far, tonight had been no different.

Brad took a sip of water, then set down his glass. "Jimmy passed the physical for the firefighting training program in Forsyth, Georgia. He leaves in six days and will be gone for ten weeks."

Erica turned to face him. "How do you feel about his career choice?"

"Surprised." Brad pushed his empty plate aside. "At least he'll always have a job."

Their waiter strode over. "Do you a want a to-go box, Ms. Nelson?"

Erica eyed the remaining food on her plate. "No thank you."

"How about dessert?"

She shook her head. "No thanks."

Brad smiled at the young man who had been one of his students a few years earlier. "We're ready for the check." After paying, he helped Erica into her lightweight jacket then escorted her out to the porch and down the steps to the sidewalk. "The weather's nice enough. What do you say we walk for a while?"

"Good idea." They turned right. Unlike previous walks, Brad didn't reach for her hand. Half a block up Main, Erica peered across the street at a swath of land where a row of stores and restaurants had once thrived. "It's sad how that fire burned down all those businesses last year. Faith and several of Blue Ridge Inn's guests watched the flames from the inn's back porch."

"Residents raised a good amount of money to help those folks."

"The same way they did for Theo."

"Have you heard from his mother?"

"Not a peep. We're assuming she moved back to Chattanooga."

After they strolled past Canoe then Anchor and Harbor, a couple Erica had met at Hilltop Inn's open house stopped to chat with them. Moments after resuming their walk, Brad stopped beside a friend sitting on a bench in front of a clothing store. After they talked about golf for a couple of minutes, the friend's wife walked out carrying a bag featuring the store's logo.

Brad and Erica resumed strolling. "Speaking of golf, Carl and Lauren invited us to play next Saturday."

"I'm game." They hadn't been with Brad and his wife's best friends since they had double-dated back in January. Erica glanced sideways at Brad's profile. Had he told Carl or Lauren about the engagement ring?

Three teenaged girls Erica remembered from the basketball game walked out of The Chocolate Express and rushed toward them. Was it her imagination, or were they swooning over their principal? After all, Abby had claimed the students, especially the girls, were crazy about their principal.

"Hey, Mr. Barkley."

"How's it going, girls?"

After chatting for a few minutes with the students, they moved on. Erica nudged Brad. "You have quite a fan club."

He chuckled. "I'm not nearly as popular as when I coached a championship football team."

They continued strolling past stores. After passing the train station and crossing the street to the park, Brad stepped off the sidewalk and headed straight to the wooden gazebo. Inside, he leaned back against the railing. His hardened expression made it clear he had something on his mind.

Erica brushed a leaf off the railing. Should she ask? Better to wait. She mirrored his stance and peered across the street at Mountain Mama's Coffee Lounge. Sometimes it seemed like only yesterday when the business was connected to Blue Ridge Inn.

Brad crossed his arms. "Do you realize you haven't said a word about the ring since the night I asked you to take it home?"

There it was. The reason his demeanor had changed. "I didn't know you expected updates." Her snarky tone accompanied the sinking sensation in the pit of Erica's stomach.

"Have you even opened the box?"

A sudden gust of wind blowing through the gazebo momentarily rendered Erica speechless.

"I'll take your silence as a no."

Erica spun around and caught sight of the courthouse a block away. If she hadn't been called to serve on jury duty, would her past have remained buried deep in her subconscious? "Do you want me to give the box back to you?"

"Depends."

"On what?"

Brad remained silent for a long moment. "Whether or not you intend to open it."

Erica squeezed her eyes shut. Were her goals the real reason she hesitated, or deep down was she afraid of another failed marriage? Brad was nothing like Jack or Gunter.

"Your silence says everything I need to know."

Erica's eyes popped open. She turned toward Brad as he pushed away from the railing. Was he seconds from walking out of her life?

"Wait!"

He spun toward her, his mouth set in a hard line.

"I just need more time."

"How much time?"

Erica shifted her weight from one leg to the other. "A month? Maybe a little longer?"

"Are you asking or answering?"

Her eyes met his. "You know I love you."

"And I need to avoid sitting across a table from the woman I love, wondering if she'll break her promise."

A knot replaced the empty sensation in Erica's stomach. "Are you breaking up with me?"

"My feelings for you haven't changed." He drew close and gently brushed a lock of hair away from her cheek. "To avoid pressuring you, I suggest we limit our time together to golf dates with Carl and Lauren."

"Safety in numbers?"

"Something like that."

Erica's focus drifted to a couple walking hand in hand on the sidewalk. "Do they know about—"

"The ring?"

"Yes."

"It's still our secret. About my suggestion?"

Her eyes returned to the man Millie had called movie-star handsome. The man whose touch filled her with desire. "I believe your idea is best for both of us."

"Until I see my ring on your finger, we're pals and golf partners." Brad gripped Erica's elbow until they stepped out of the gazebo. They strode across the grass to the sidewalk then headed back the way they had come. Her arm brushed his shoulder as they crossed the side street. How much longer would his patience last? They strode past a family walking out of The Sweet Shoppe. Five steps past Owl's Nest, Brad's fingers curled around her hand, sending a wave of desire coursing through her. How much longer could she resist wearing his ring?

They returned to his Corvette. Erica lowered onto the passenger seat while Brad hastened to the driver's side. She glanced sideways at him as he pulled out of the parking space. Should she start a conversation? Would her heart and her mind align the moment she achieved her goals? Brad turned on the radio, a clear indication he wasn't in the mood to talk. After parking on the ranch house driveway, he walked Erica to her door. Would he kiss her? She faced him. "About tonight—"

He pressed his finger to her lips. "We'll talk in a few days." He kissed her forehead, then spun around and headed back to his car.

Erica's heart yearned to rush after him and tell him how much she loved him, but her mind refused to give into her heart. She unlocked the door and stepped inside.

Amanda looked up from the den sofa. "How's Brad?"

If she shared details about the evening, she'd probably break down in tears. "He's fine. I have a lot on my plate tomorrow, so I'm turning in."

"I'll see you in the morning."

Erica headed straight to her room and closed the door, conflicting thoughts about the evening playing havoc with her emotions. Moments after she changed into pajamas, her heart overruled her mind. She opened the dresser drawer. Her fingers wrapped around the black box. If she peeked, would her commitment to achieving her number one goal dissolve? Only one way to find out.

Erica removed the box from the drawer. Her heart pounded against her ribs as she opened the lid. She stared at the diamond set in gold. The stone shimmered as she gently removed the ring and held it up to the light. Had Brad selected a two or a three-carat diamond? Of all the eligible women in Blue Ridge, he had fallen in love with her. Maybe the time had come to readjust her goal.

Erica placed the ring back into the box, vowing to ask Brad to slip it onto her finger sometime before spring gave way to summer.

Chapter 30

Wendy lowered her little guy into his playpen at the end of the kitchen counter. "What do you think? Should we have spaghetti or chicken for supper?"

Ryan babbled a response while gripping the edge and pulling up to his feet.

Wendy giggled. "Definitely spaghetti. Especially since I have exciting news to share with your daddy after dinner." She removed a container of sauce from the fridge and set a water-filled pasta pot on the stove, then handed a sippy cup to her little guy. He wrapped his fingers around a handle and took a sip before dropping onto his diaper-padded fanny. "In a few months we'll celebrate your first birthday with a big party and a special cake baked by your Grammy Millie. One day when you're old enough to understand, I'll explain our unique family tree."

The garage door opening sent Duke scrambling to the back door and Wendy to the window. "Your daddy's home."

"Dada." Ryan dropping his cup and pulling up to his feet warmed Wendy's heart. "You love your daddy, don't you?"

Chris swung the back door open, patted Duke, then pulled Wendy into his arms. "Italian night?"

She wrapped her fingers around his neck. "Blue Ridge style."

"My favorite." He kissed Wendy's cheek then released her and scooped Ryan into his arms. "How's my boy?"

Duke padded behind Chris as he carried his son to the other end of the great room. The first time Chris brought her to his home, she'd sipped nonalcoholic wine out on the deck while watching the setting sun paint multiple shades of orange and pink across the western sky. That night she couldn't imagine him falling in love with her. Amazing how much had changed during the past year.

Wendy dropped spaghetti noodles into the boiling water and set the timer, then prepared a Caesar salad with bottled dressing. Despite Millie's encouragement, cooking remained far down her list of favorite activities. Sharing exciting news with Chris was near the top. She carried salad bowls to the table, then prepared a plate of bite-sized chicken and fruit for her little guy.

The timer buzzed, sending Wendy to the stove. She drained and plated the noodles, added sauce, and sprinkled on shredded parmesan. "Dinner's ready for my two favorite guys."

"We're coming." Chris placed his son in his high chair, then pulled out a chair for Wendy while Duke sprawled beside Ryan.

Wendy smiled. "Your daddy is a perfect gentleman." Chris kissed the back of her neck, sending a wave of desire coursing through her limbs. Her eyes followed him as he settled across from her. Maybe she should tell him during dinner. He reached across the table for her hand. She closed her eyes. A smile curled Wendy's lips as she listened to the man who had captured her heart thanking God for His blessings. She'd wait until they were alone to share the news.

"Amen." After releasing Wendy's hand, Chris motioned toward the candles on the table. "Are we celebrating a special event?"

Wendy tilted her head. "Isn't every day a celebration?"

"With you, yes." Chris swirled spaghetti around his fork and tasted. "Delicious. Especially for a gal who doesn't like to cook."

Turning on her charm and her best southern accent, Wendy fanned her face. "The sacrifices I make for my handsome hero."

Chris laughed. "Well worth the effort, Miss Scarlett."

Wendy's mind drifted to eight months earlier when Chris had introduced her to *Gone with the Wind*. She had watched the movie twice since that night. "Why thank you, dahlin' Rhett." She stabbed a piece of lettuce. "His best line in the whole movie was 'You should be kissed, and often, and by someone who knows how.'"

Chris winked while tilting his water glass toward Wendy. "I'll demonstrate later tonight."

"If I said I was madly in love with you, I'd be telling the truth, and what's more, you'd know it."

"Another line from the movie?"

"Uh-huh. Except I changed the word lie to truth."

"Lucky me."

A car engine pulling in front of their home perked Duke's ears seconds before he scrambled to the front door.

Wendy's brow pinched. "Are you expecting someone?"

Chris shook his head. "Probably a delivery." Responding to the bell, he rose and opened the front door. "Kayla?"

Wendy rushed to Chris's side. "Why didn't you let us know you were coming?" She embraced her sister.

"I wanted to surprise you."

"Mission accomplished." Releasing Kayla, Wendy peered over her sister's shoulder. "Did Harper or another friend drive you?"

"I sort of drove by myself...in Mom's car."

"Two months ago you only had a learner's permit." Wendy's brow pinched as she eyed her sister's sheepish expression. "You're not old enough to have a permanent license, are you?"

Kayla shrugged. "Doesn't matter. I know how to drive."

Chris swung the door closed. "Are you aware that you've broken the law, young lady?"

"It's not like I robbed a bank or something."

Chris stared at her. "What happens when your parents discover your mother's car is missing?"

"I guess they'll think someone stole it." Kayla's eyes widened. "You're not gonna turn me in, are you?"

"As an attorney, I'm obligated to report crimes."

Wendy stared at Chris. Was he fibbing to scare Kayla?

"Unless you're my lawyer, right?"

"Since you know about attorney-client privilege, you should be smart enough to understand that driving a block, much less several hundred miles without a license, could land you in a heap of trouble." Chris's tone was firm.

Kayla's lip trembled. "Is ten dollars enough to hire you?"

"More than enough." Wendy linked arms with her sister. "Are you hungry?"

"Kind of."

"I'll fix you a plate."

Chris pulled a chair out for his sister-in-law then returned to his chair and faced Kayla. "After we finish dinner, you need to tell us why you left home."

"Okay."

Wendy kept a close eye on Kayla's slumped shoulders while plating her dinner. Chris had been right to scold her for making such a foolish decision. What if she had caused an accident or run off the road and landed upside down in a ditch? Fortunately nothing bad had happened. At least not yet. "One serving of spaghetti and salad coming up." Wendy set the plates in front of her sister, then lowered onto her chair. Her eyes met Chris's. They both understood Kayla had put them in a precarious position. The question was why. Unsure what to say, Wendy swirled spaghetti around her fork.

Ryan broke the silence with a giggle while dropping a piece of chicken on the floor, which prompted Duke to fill his role as their canine cleanup crew. Wendy touched her little guy's arm. "Our doggie's all full now, honey." Desperate to ease the tension, her focus shifted to her husband. "How'd everything go today?"

His jaw tightened. "As expected." He obviously wasn't in the mood for chitchat. The uncomfortable silence resumed and continued until Kayla swallowed her last bite. Chris carried the empty plates to the kitchen sink then returned to the table and faced his new client. "Time for you to explain to your attorney why you broke the law."

Kayla picked at her fingernail. "Mom knows."

"That you stole her car?"

She shook her head. "That I've connected with you and Wendy."

Chris crossed his arms on the table. "How'd she find out?"

"Last night, Mom fixed us dinner for the first time in a couple of weeks. We got to talking about some of the celebrities who had come into Gilmores during the past month. Tim McGraw. Amy Grant. Keith Urban. They like hearing Dad's music." Her brow pinched. "That's when it happened." She hesitated.

Wendy reached across the table and touched Kayla's hand. "You can tell us. We'll understand."

"Dad asked me when I was gonna bring Wendy and Chris back to the bar." Her eyes met Wendy's. "Mom asked Wendy who."

"Your dad said Armstrong, didn't he?"

Kayla nodded. "I've never seen Mom so angry. She accused me of going behind her back to destroy our family. Dad didn't have a clue what was going on. Especially after Mom made my sister and brother go upstairs to their rooms, then left me alone with him. I had to explain everything to him." Her eyes turned red. "That's the first time I'd seen my daddy cry."

Wendy swallowed the lump rising in her throat as she scooted her chair closer to her sister. "Then what happened?"

"He left to go back to Gilmore's. This morning his car was still gone, and Mom was still in their bedroom. I skipped school, hoping to apologize to her. She never came out." Tears pooled and slid down Kayla's cheeks. "Now she hates both of us."

Wendy wrapped her arm around her sister's shoulder. "She could never hate you, honey."

Chris nodded. "Wendy's right."

Kayla swiped her fingers across her cheeks. "Can I stay here with you and Wendy?"

"Until tomorrow, then we'll figure out how to get you home." Chris uncrossed his arms. "Now you're going to call your father and tell him where you are."

"What if he doesn't know I'm gone?"

"He will when you tell him."

"Since you're my lawyer, is it okay if I put him on speaker?"

The corner of Chris's mouth curved up. "As one of my favorite clients, yeah, it's okay."

Kayla hesitated, then pulled her phone from her back pocket. She stared at the screen. "Three missed calls from Dad. Guess I shouldn't have silenced my phone." She punched a number, then activated the speaker.

Brent Gilmore answered before the first ring ended. "Kayla. Thank God. Where are you?"

"In Blue Ridge with Wendy and Chris. Is Mom okay?"

"She's worried sick."

Kayla's tears returned. "I'm sorry I ran away, Daddy."

"I understand, honey. Truth is I should've stayed home last night to help you and your mother deal with the situation."

Wendy leaned close to the phone. "Chris and I will make sure Kayla returns home safe and sound tomorrow."

"Do you mind if I make hotel reservations for you tomorrow night so I can thank you with dinner at Gilmore's?"

Wendy caught Chris's eye. He nodded.

"All right."

"I'll text Kayla the information. In the meantime, thank you for taking care of my daughter."

"She's my sister and my little guy's aunt." Wendy smiled at Kayla. "We take care of family."

As soon as the call ended, Chris lifted Ryan from the high chair. "Your cousin will keep you company while your mommy and I take care of all these plates." He motioned for Kayla to follow him, then returned to the kitchen and pulled Wendy aside. "I'll be tied up in court for the next three days."

"I know." She plucked her phone off the counter and pressed Amanda's number.

"Hey, what's up?"

"You won't believe what happened." Wendy carried her phone into the office. Twenty minutes later, she returned. The table had been cleared. Kayla sat on the floor in front of the fireplace with Ryan while Chris closed the dishwasher and pressed the start button. Wendy moved beside him. "Thank you for cleaning up, darling."

"Glad to help. What's the plan?"

"I'll drive Cynthia's car, and Amanda will follow in the truck. Your mom will take care of Ryan."

"Well done." Chris wrapped his arms around Wendy. "When was the last time I told you how much I love you?"

"Hmm. A couple of days ago?" She gazed deep into his eyes. The time seemed right. "Come with me." Wendy led him to their office and closed the door.

"Are we hiding from our surprise guest for a romantic moment?"

"Not exactly." Wendy ran her fingers along the top of her desk. "You know that big unfinished space in the basement?"

"What about it?"

She faced Chris, smiling. "How long do you think it will take to build an office down there?"

Their eyes met. "The cowgirl hat. That night at Gaylord." His lips curled into a smile. "You're pregnant, aren't you?"

Wendy laced her fingers around his neck. "We have a little more than seven months to transform this room into a nursery."

Chris wrapped his arms around Wendy and kissed her. For the moment, despite her runaway little sister sitting in their great room, all seemed right with the world.

Chapter 31

After stashing her suitcase behind the back seat beside Kayla's duffel bag, Wendy slid onto the late-model SUV's driver's seat. She typed the Gilmores' home address into Waze, then secured her phone in the holder and peered at her sister sitting beside her. Kayla had barely spoken a word since she'd awakened an hour and a half earlier. "Are you ready to go?"

Kayla's focus remained locked on her phone. "I guess so."

Wendy gripped the steering wheel. "All right, then. Next stop Nashville." She backed up and turned around then eased down the driveway. Amanda following them in the truck triggered memories of their caravan from New Orleans to Asheville after they'd learned the truth about Gunter. Morgan had taken the lead in the rental truck filled with their remaining possessions. Amanda followed in Gunter's truck, one of three vehicles that hadn't been repossessed. That day she had no idea Kayla existed. Wendy glanced at her sister's thumbs tapping her phone. "Do you mind if we listen to music?"

"Is country western okay?"

"Absolutely."

Kayla tapped the dashboard screen then refocused on her phone.

So much for conversation. Hoping to fill the void, Wendy hummed along with familiar tunes. A mile away from Chattanooga, Kayla heaved a heavy sigh. Wendy reached across the console and touched her arm. "Are you okay?"

"Last night after you and Chris went to bed, I called Dad."

Wendy lowered the music volume. "I imagine he's eager to have you home."

Kayla leaned back against the headrest. "I told him I deserved to know the truth about Mom's health."

"What'd he say?"

"He'd talk to her. She's obviously the one holding out."

Typical. Wendy swallowed the retort threatening to escape. Commenting about Cynthia's insensitivity wouldn't help her sister deal with reality. "One of these days, she'll come around."

"According to Dad, she hasn't told my sister and brother about you."

Wendy's grip on the steering wheel tightened. *Why would she? In her mind I don't exist.* Relieved she hadn't blurted the comment aloud, Wendy loosened her grip. "One more secret she has to deal with. Speaking of secrets, I shared some news with my Blue Ridge family before we left."

Kayla lifted her head off the headrest. "About me?"

"No, but in a way you're involved." Her sister's wide-eyed expression brought a smile to Wendy's face. "Before the end of the year, you'll have another niece or nephew."

"Cool. Did you get pregnant when you and Chris were in Nashville?"

"So it seems."

"If we lived closer, I could babysit."

"After you have a permanent driver's license, and if your parents approve, you could visit us during your summer break."

"I could spend the whole summer with you." Responding to her pinging phone, Kayla ended the conversation. Her focus remained glued to her phone until they were minutes away from her home. "Dad picked a fancy hotel close to Gilmore's for you and Amanda. You should go to the Country Music Hall of Fame while you're here."

"Good idea." Wendy's shoulders stiffened as she turned onto the Gilmores' street. "How do think your mother will respond if she sees her car?"

"She won't come outside."

Because you're with me, the rejected daughter. Wendy pressed her lips tight to resist making a snide remark. The Gilmore home came into view. She pulled onto the driveway and parked in front of the garage. "I hope she doesn't give you too hard a time."

"Mom will probably ignore me until I turn eighteen." Kayla's tone hinted of pain.

Wendy's heart ached for her sister. "Do you want me to go in with you?"

"She's already furious with me. Seeing you would send her over the edge." Kayla gripped her door handle. "Thanks for letting me stay an extra day with you and Chris."

"We always enjoy spending time with you."

"Me too."

Wendy opened the rear hatch, then headed to the back of the SUV.

Kayla sidled beside her. "I'll see you tonight at Gilmore's."

"You promised to play the piano the next time I visited."

"Yeah, I know."

"I hope you'll keep your promise."

Kayla slid her phone into her back pocket. "I'll think about it."

"Fair enough." Wendy pulled her sister into an embrace. "I love you and I'll always be here for you."

"I love you too." Kayla sniffled. "I'll play for you tonight."

Wendy released her, smiling. "I can't wait."

While Kayla headed to the sidewalk leading to the front porch, Wendy set her suitcase on the driveway and released the handle. Would Cynthia ever acknowledge the relationship that had developed between her two oldest daughters? She heaved a heavy sigh then pulled her suitcase to the end of the driveway and stowed it on the truck's back seat. After slamming the door closed, she climbed in beside Amanda.

"Good thing you didn't break the rear window."

"Sorry." Wendy punched a new address into Waze. "Next stop, Omni Hotel."

***

Amanda shifted the truck into drive. "Are you aware that someone was watching from an upstairs window?"

Wendy's head jerked toward her. "Cynthia?"

"I couldn't tell." Amanda eased away from the curb. "Did you learn anything new during the past few hours?"

"Not much." Wendy's shoulders slumped. "Except a confirmation that Cynthia hasn't changed."

"Did you expect her to?"

"I'd hoped she had, for Kayla's sake. My sister spent most of the trip glued to her phone."

"Typical teenager."

"If I had listened to Chris and refused to go to her dad's bar and restaurant, Kayla wouldn't have to deal with her mother's anger."

"Maybe Cynthia will have a change of heart."

Wendy scoffed. "Fat chance of that ever happening."

"Hey, what happened to your cheerleader attitude?"

"My mother snuffed it out, that's what." Wendy's tone reeked of disgust. "How about we change the subject to something fun."

"Good idea. Congratulations again on your good news."

"Thanks."

"Are you dealing with morning sickness?"

Wendy's brows raised. "You call that positive?"

"I need to know what to expect when we wake up in the same room tomorrow morning."

"You'll be happy to know that the only time I dealt with nausea when I was pregnant with Ryan was the morning after the blizzard." Wendy chuckled. "Do you suppose that bout of morning sickness was punishment for conning you and Erica into helping me build dozens of miniature snowmen on Blue Ridge Inn's front porch?"

"Definitely." They continued chatting about the blizzard until Amanda pulled under the Omni Hotel canopy and turned the truck over to valet.

Inside the lobby, the gentleman at the check-in desk handed Wendy an envelope from Kayla's father. She pulled out two tickets for the Country Music Hall of Fame along with a folded sheet of paper. She opened the note. "He says, '*Welcome back to Nashville. The Hall of Fame is around the corner. Gilmore's Bar and Restaurant is three blocks from the hotel. Kayla and I will meet you there at six.*'"

"We might as well play tourist while we're here. Who knows?" Amanda linked arms with Wendy. "Maybe I'll turn into a country-western fan." They made their way to the elevators and rode to the eighth floor. Moments after entering their room, Amanda pulled her phone from her purse. "It's Erica." She pressed the speaker icon. "Hey, we just walked into our hotel room."

"Are you both listening?" Her tone hinted of angst.

"We are." Amanda sat on the edge of the bed closest to the window.

Wendy dropped onto the bed across from her, her brow pinched. "What's going on?"

"Jillian called a few minutes ago. Sierra wants to take Theo back."

"Are you kidding me?" Amanda stared at her phone. "She drops her newborn on a doorstep, and now she considers herself a fit mother?"

"Jillian will schedule a bench hearing with family court to let a judge decide whether or not to grant her custody. In the meantime, she'll accompany Sierra for a supervised weekly visit."

"I can't imagine a judge siding with her." Amanda eyed the white swirls and circles on the gray carpet. The perfect symbols for the chaos Theo's mother had created. "How's Abby taking the news?"

"She doesn't know yet."

Wendy lifted off the bed and ambled to the window.

Following a short conversation, Amanda ended the call and moved beside Wendy. "Are you okay?"

"I understand why you and Erica don't believe Sierra deserves to have her son back in her life." Wendy turned away from the window. "But at least she cares enough to want him."

Chapter 32

Following an afternoon of playing tourist, Wendy and Amanda stepped out of the elevator at lobby level and headed toward the front entrance. She pulled her pinging phone from her purse. "Kayla texted. She'll meet us at Gilmore's in five minutes."

"Hopefully, we're close."

"We're three blocks away." Wendy dropped her phone back into her purse. Outside, the sun hovering above the horizon failed to warm the cool air. She zipped up her jacket. "I hope Kayla's in a happier mood than she was during our drive."

"Whatever her mood, you need to turn on your Wendy charm."

Wendy nudged Amanda's arm. "Two cheerleaders are better than one."

"Yeah, but you're the squad leader." They stopped at an intersection. "Have you heard Mr. Gilmore's band?"

"No, but Kayla says they're the best in Nashville."

"A totally biased opinion. What's he like?"

Wendy shrugged. "He's charming and sociable."

"Excellent qualities for a bar owner."

The light changed. At the next intersection they turned the corner. Wendy's pulse accelerated, the same as it had the first time she had approached Gilmore's. At least tonight she wouldn't have to worry about Kayla's father discovering her true identity.

As promised, Kayla met them at the entrance. She led them to a table in the corner as the guest band announced a ten-minute break. Wendy peeled out of her jacket then sat facing the stage. Kayla settled in on Wendy's right. "Dad's band plays at eight."

Amanda hung her purse on the back of the chair next to the brick wall. "I hear his band is exceptional."

"Especially when he plays his own music."

The waitress who had served Wendy and Chris months earlier ambled over. "Welcome back to Gilmore's."

"Thank you." Had she remembered, or had her boss clued her in?

"May I bring you something from the bar?"

Wendy pressed her hand to her belly. "Ginger ale on the rocks for me."

Amanda scooted her chair closer to the table. "A glass of chardonnay."

"Coming right up, along with Kayla's favorite mocktail."

"On second thought." Wendy peered up at the young woman. "Bring me what you're bringing Kayla."

"Excellent choice."

The good-looking, middle-aged man wearing cowboy boots, jeans, and a plaid shirt approached. "Welcome back, Wendy."

"Thank you. Meet Amanda, my dear friend and my little guy's honorary grandmother."

Amanda offered him her hand. "It's a pleasure to meet you, Mr. Gilmore."

"Likewise." He smiled while releasing her hand. "Given Wendy is my daughter's half-sister and you're her son's grandmother, Mr. Gilmore is far too formal. Please, call me Brent." He sat facing Wendy. "I hope you ladies enjoyed the Hall of Fame."

"So much so that Amanda is on her way to becoming a country-music fan."

"When in Nashville—" He pulled a phone from his pocket and eyed the screen. "I need to take this call." He stood and walked away with his phone pressed to his ear.

Their waitress returned with their drinks. "Are you ladies ready to order, or do you want to wait for Mr. Gilmore to return?"

Kayla wrapped her fingers around her glass. "We'll wait for Dad."

"I'll bring you bread and smoked trout dip to tide you over." Their waitress smiled then walked away.

Wendy tasted her mocktail. "Great choice, Kayla." She took a second sip, then set her glass down. "Did you talk to your mother after I dropped you off?"

Kayla shook her head. "I stayed in my room until Dad came home to drive me here." She broke eye contact as she twirled her straw in her drink. "What'd you do this afternoon?"

Wendy eyed Kayla's downcast eyes. Her sister obviously didn't want to talk about their mother. "We had a great day…" Kayla perked up the moment Wendy began talking about their Hall of Fame experience.

They discussed exhibits and shared their favorite inductee while they listened to the guest band and nibbled on the appetizer. Until Amanda stopped mid-sentence, her jaw slack.

Wendy touched Amanda's arm. "What's wrong?"

"She's here."

"Who?"

"Your mother."

Startled, Wendy jerked her head around.

Brent gripped Cynthia's elbow as they closed the distance to their table. Despite being noticeably thinner, Cynthia could still turn heads. He seated her across from Wendy, then turned and walked away.

Cynthia's eyes shifted from Kayla to Wendy. "We need to talk."

Wendy's back stiffened. Was the woman, who anyone watching could tell was her mother, seconds from demanding she end her relationship with Kayla? "If you're angry at your daughter—"

"Please." Cynthia aimed her palm at Wendy. "Let me say what I need to say."

Wendy's shoulders tightened. So much for talking. "I'm listening."

Cynthia turned toward Kayla. "This morning my heart broke the moment I saw you and Wendy embracing in our driveway."

Wendy stole a quick glance at Amanda. The person in the window was her mother.

"I've never been a praying woman...until today. I spent hours on my knees, crying a river of tears, and asking God to forgive me for the unmotherly way I've treated all my children." Cynthia's focus shifted from Kayla to Wendy. "Abandoning my little girl, then rejecting her when she came to our home last year was cruel and selfish."

A multitude of thoughts collided in Wendy's head. Was her mother seeking absolution?

Cynthia grasped Kayla's hand. "So was shielding you from the truth about my health."

"You're real sick, aren't you?" Kayla's voice trembled.

"I'm afraid so." Cynthia's eyes reddened. "I've been diagnosed with stage-four cancer."

"Are you going to die?"

"Try not to worry about me, sweetheart." Her mother stroked her child's hand. "I've made peace with my Savior. Soon I'll slip from this world to my eternal home."

Tears slid down Kayla's cheeks. "How long before—"

"Six months, maybe more." Cynthia stretched her other hand toward Wendy.

Tears erupted the moment her mother's fingers wrapped around her hand. All these years without her, and now she was months away from losing her?

"God is giving me time to renew my relationship with you while becoming acquainted with the only grandchild I'll ever have the opportunity to love."

"Two grandchildren. My second baby will be born in October."

A smile that could only be explained as pure joy lit her mother's face. "I love you, Wendy, and I promise to live long enough to hold my new grandchild in my arms."

Praying God's grace would allow her mother to keep her promise, Wendy swiped her fingers across her cheeks. "I love you...Mom."

"Will you forgive me for abandoning you all those years ago?"

The pain that had held Wendy captive for the past nineteen years melted away. "With all my heart."

Her mother squeezed her hand. "I couldn't be prouder of you and Kayla."

"I promised Wendy I'd play the piano for her tonight." Kayla sniffled as she dabbed at her tears. "Will you sing one of Daddy's songs while I play?"

"I'd be honored to." Her mother released Wendy's hand then accompanied her second oldest daughter onto the stage and waited for the song to end. The lead singer turned toward her. She whispered in his ear. He nodded, then stepped aside. The woman who had walked away from her five-year-old child stepped up to the microphone. "Ladies and gentlemen, my daughter Kayla and I would like to dedicate this next song, which was written by my husband, Brent, to my first-born child." She turned toward their table. "This is for you, my darling Wendy."

Amanda's eyes teared up as she reached across the corner of the table and held Wendy's hand. "This is one of the most beautiful moments I have ever experienced."

Wendy placed her hand over Amanda's. "She loves me," she whispered, her voice filled with awe. "My mother truly loves me."

"With all her heart."

The words of the song poured out, weaving a story of love, regret, and longing that could only have been written by someone who understood the breakdown and mending of a family. As her mother's voice lingered in the air, Wendy understood she would carry the melody with her forever.

Thank you for reading book five in what will be the multi-book Blue Ridge Series. Book six, Summer of Second Chances will publish in June. The eBook is available for preorder.

If you aren't already one of my newsletter friends and would like to stay updated on my releases and other fun information, become a subscriber and I'll send you a link to my standalone romance, Jenny's Grace:

Afterword

When I first envisioned writing a series about three strangers meeting at a historic inn in a small town, Blue Ridge, Georgia seemed the perfect setting. Since publishing *Blizzard at Blue Ridge Inn*, Tim and I have visited the town twice. During the first, I participated in a book signing at the real Blue Ridge Inn, and at Owl's Nest on East Main Street. The second time we visited our new friends and shopped for Christmas gifts.

As Wendy's, Erica's, and Amanda's lives evolved I knew this would become a multi-book series. I'm currently writing book six. *Summer of Second Chances*, and already know what will happen in book seven. Both books will also publish in 2025, with more titles coming in 2026.

In the meantime, I look forward to our next visit to Blue Ridge to enjoy restaurants we haven't yet tried and experience new adventures.

Acknowledgements

Little did I know when my first book published in 2018 how many wonderful old and new friends would join me on this journey.

My editor, Sherri Stewart is a wonderful partner who overcomes my punctuation challenges and inspires me to take my work to new levels. Elaina Lee, my cover designer has created all of my current covers. Both women are a joy to work with.

My beta readers, Pat Davis, Bev Feldkamp, Carlene Dunn, Kitty Metzger, Kathy Warner, CJ Bruce, Zanase Duncan, and Lynn Worley provided excellent feedback and suggestions for *The Promise*. My dedicated launch team members are the first to post reviews, which help new readers discover my series. My newsletter friends and readers' loyalty make my heart sing.

A special thank you to my amazing family for encouraging me and helping me prove it's never too late to follow your dreams.

Above all I'm grateful to God for His amazing grace and the gift of eternal life through Jesus.

www.ingramcontent.com/pod-product-compliance
Lightning Source LLC
LaVergne TN
LVHW041916070526
838199LV00051BA/2635